CHINESE FABLES
Supplementary Chinese Reader Vol.10

編著者／方祖燊・黃迺毓
by Tzu-shen Fang
   Nai-yu Huang

中國寓言故事

中國語文補充讀物 十

國立編譯館主編
正中書局印行

前言

　　中國古籍中的寓言故事雖然很多，但要選擇適合外國人士和華僑子弟讀，又富有教育意義的卻也不多，再加上要把那些簡短的原作，改寫成既淺白又有趣味的故事，也並不是一件簡單的事情。雖然如此，但我們總想把它編寫得更好，所以在這些短短的文章中，加一些描寫，來增加一些文學的意味；加一些同樣句型的文字，希望外國人士與華僑子弟，能夠由這些句型，熟悉我國文字的用法。

　　我們在這本中國寓言故事裡，收了二十篇作品，內容的安排，大抵採用國立編譯館中國語文補充讀物的體制，包括故事本文、字詞解釋與例句、成語解釋與例句、句型舉例，練習（有詞語造句與回答問題兩種）。我們希望學習華文的人，能夠由此知道中國的一些趣聞故事，神話傳說，瞭解一些中國人的生活態度，愛情觀念，哲學思想，民間習俗，而且希望對於他們講華語、寫中文，也能夠有一些幫助。附錄有「詞類略語表」、「中文一千個最常用字表」、「本書字和詞索引」，以便學者參考翻查。這本小書，讀華語華文中級班的外籍人士、華僑子弟，如果用作課本，應該是很適合的。

方祖燊　黃迺毓
中華民國八十五年七月

Forward

Although there are quite a few fables among ancient Chinese books, it is not easy to choose some for foreigners or overseas Chinese to read or study. They should be simple, educational, and interesting. However, we tried to make them better by adding some descriptions in order to have more literary flavor. We also used repeated sentence patterns for readers to get familiar with the Chinese sentence pattern.

In this volume, we collected twenty fables. As for the arrangement of the context, we used the pattern set similar to the supplementary Chinese Reader by the National Institute for Compilation and Tranlation. Following each text are vocabulary, idiomatic expressions, sentence patterns and exercises. After reading this book, we hope that readers who want to learn Chinese will read some interesting stories, myths, and legends; understand the Chinese viewpoint of living, love, philosophy, and customs; and learn to speak and write better Chinese. The " Grammatical Notations " " List of 1000 Characters Commonly Used " and " vocabulary used in this volume " are included in the appendix for reference. This book is suitable as a textbook in a medium Chinese class for foreigners and overseas Chinese students.

Tzuu-shen Fang
Nai-yu Huang

July, 1996

目　次

前　言
第一課　　殺雞取卵 …………………………………… 1
第二課　　溫柔的月姊兒 ……………………………… 13
第三課　　美姿巧舌 …………………………………… 23
第四課　　點石成金 …………………………………… 37
第五課　　不要隨便跟人開玩笑 ……………………… 47
第六課　　狡兔三窟 …………………………………… 61
第七課　　擡驢進城 …………………………………… 69
第八課　　井底之蛙 …………………………………… 81
第九課　　害人反害己 ………………………………… 93
第十課　　尋求真理 …………………………………… 109
第十一課　除禍要趁早 ………………………………… 123
第十二課　致富之術 …………………………………… 137
第十三課　忘恩負義 …………………………………… 149
第十四課　不合時宜的詩人 …………………………… 159
第十五課　小魚的快樂 ………………………………… 173
第十六課　知音難求 …………………………………… 183

第十七課	替貓取別號 ……………………	195
第十八課	狗和稻子 ………………………	205
第十九課	比唱山歌 ………………………	219
第二十課	梅花的故事 ……………………	231
附錄一	詞類略語表 ……………………	243
附錄二	世界中文報業協會三千個基本常用字彙表中的一千個最常用字 ……………	245
附錄三	本冊所用生字表 ………………	257
附錄四	本冊生字與生詞索引 …………	265

第一課　殺雞取卵

　　有一對夫婦養了一隻大母雞，每天生一個小小的金蛋。這是天帝憐憫他們年紀老，無力工作，因此給了他們這麼一隻會生金蛋的母雞，讓他們每天有固定的收入，可以買吃的穿的，生活雖然不算頂富足，但也可以過得去了。

　　但是這一對老夫婦，總覺得一天只有一個小小的金蛋，花起來不夠痛快，要想買大魚大肉吃，要想買時髦新款式的衣服穿，要想買珠花玉鐲來戴，要想到世界各地旅遊觀光，就不夠支出了。他們想：「這隻母雞既然能夠不斷地生金蛋，一定滿肚子裏裝的都是金蛋，何不把牠給殺了，全都拿出來，花個痛快；這麼一來，我們不就一下子變成大富翁了嗎？那時

2　中國寓言故事

候，愛怎麼花就怎麼花錢，再也不受什麼限制了。」

夫婦倆一商量，就把這隻母雞殺了。剖開肚子一看，裏面還有七八個金蛋。就這麼幾個金蛋，他們很快也就花光了。從此，他們再也沒有了收入，生活過得非常困苦。

他們不知道「將本求利」的道理；本錢存在，才能夠不斷滋生利息來花用，要是一下子把老本兒都用光了，又那能再生出利息來呢？

Ⅰ. 生字與生詞

1. **夫婦**（ㄈㄨ ㄈㄨˋ；fūfù）

    N：husband and wife；married couple
    那一對夫婦只有一個孩子
    The couple have only one child.
    夫：a husband；a man；
    婦：a woman；a wife；a married woman

2. **憐憫**（ㄌㄧㄢˊ ㄇㄧㄣˇ；liánmǐn）

    TV：to take pity on... to feel or show sorrow or pity for；to sympathize with
    SV：merciful

3. **年紀**（ㄋㄧㄢˊ ㄐㄧˋ；niánji）

    N：a person's age
    他們的年紀不小了。
    They are not young.

4. **因此**（ㄧㄣ ㄘˇ；yīntsž）

    MA：because of this（＝therefore）

5. **固定**（ㄍㄨˋ ㄉㄧㄥˋ；gùdìng）

    SV：fixed；firm
    FV：to fix
    固定（的）AT：regular；fixed
    他沒有固定的工作。
    He has no regular work.

6. 收入（ㄕㄡ ㄖㄨˋ；shōurù）

   N：income；earnings
   小李沒有固定的收入，因此她不想嫁給他。
   Shiau Li doesn't have a regular income, so she doesn't want to marry him.

7. 頂 （ㄉㄧㄥˇ；dǐng）

   A：topmost；extremely；very
   你的國語說得頂好。
   Your Mandarin is very good.
   他夢想有一天能住在山頂上。
   He's dreaming that one day he'll be able to live on top of a mountain.

8. 富足 （ㄈㄨˋ ㄗㄨˊ；fùtzú）

   SV：rich；wealthy；abundant

9. 痛快 （ㄊㄨㄥˋ ㄎㄨㄞˋ；tùngkuài）

   SV：to one's heart's content；happy；satisfied
   他們跳舞跳得很痛快。
   They danced to their heart's content, without mincing matters.

10. 時髦 （ㄕˊ ㄇㄠˊ；shŕmáu）

    SV：fashionable；stylish
    N：Vogue
    她是一位很時髦的女性。
    She's a very fashionable woman.

She is very stylish.

11. 新款式 （ㄒㄧㄣ ㄎㄨㄢˇ ㄕˋ; shīnkuǎnshr̀）

   N：the latest；the newest style
   這頂帽子是最新的款式。
   This hat is of the latest fashion.

12. 珠花 （ㄓㄨ ㄏㄨㄚ; jūhūa）

   N：hair decoration of pearl
   a kind of pearl head ornament
   她在頭髮上插了一個珠花作為飾物。
   She wore a flower of pearls on her hair as an ornament.

13. 玉鐲 （ㄩˋ ㄓㄨㄛˊ; yùjuó）

   N：a jade bracelet
   鐲子：a bracelet

14. 旅遊 （ㄌㄩˇ ㄧㄡˊ; liǔyóu）

   FV　N：to go touring

15. 觀光 （ㄍㄨㄢ ㄍㄨㄤ; guānguāng）

   FV：to go sightseeing
   N：sightseeing
   觀光客　N：tourist
   台灣有很多日本觀光客。
   There are many Japanese tourists in Taiwan.

16. 支出 （ㄓ ㄔㄨ; jrchū）

   N：expense；expenditure

FV：to spend；to payout
只有這一點錢，怎夠支出？
How can this little bit of money cover the expenses?

17. 富翁 （ㄈㄨˋ ㄨㄥ；fùwēng）

    N：a rich man

18. 限制 （ㄒㄧㄢˋ ㄓˋ；shiànjr̀）

    FV：to restrict；to set limit to...
    N：restrictions；control
    他媽媽限制他，一天只能花兩百塊錢。
    His mother restricted him to spending only 200 dollars a day.

19. 商量 （ㄕㄤ ㄌㄧㄤˊ；shāngliáng）

    FV：to exchange opinions or views；to confer；to discuss
    他跟他太太商量女兒出嫁的事。
    He discussed their daughter's marriage with his wife.

20. 剖開 （ㄆㄡˇ ㄎㄞ；pǒukāi）

    RE：to cut；to open

21. 花光 （ㄏㄨㄚ ㄍㄨㄤ；huāguāng）

    RE：use up (money)

22. 困苦 （ㄎㄨㄣˋ ㄎㄨˇ；kuènkǔ）

    SV：in great distress；poverty
    我們的生活很困苦。
    Our life is very difficult.

23. 道理 （ㄉㄠˋ ㄌㄧˇ；dàulǐ）
    N：reason；rationality；sensibility
    你說的很有道理。
    What you say makes a lot of sense.

24. 本錢 （ㄅㄣˇ ㄑㄧㄢˊ；běnchián）
    N：capital；investment.

25. 存在 （ㄘㄨㄣˊ ㄗㄞˋ；tsuéntzài）
    FV：to exist
    N：existence
    你相信這世界上真的有鬼存在嗎？
    Do you really believe in the existence of ghosts in the world?

26. 能夠 （ㄋㄥˊ ㄍㄡˋ；nénggòu）
    AV：Can；be able to；capable of
    我希望你能夠了解我。
    I hope you can understand me.

27. 滋生 （ㄗ ㄕㄥ；tzshēng）
    FV：to multiply；to reproduce in large numbers
    蚊子在夏天比較容易滋生。
    It's easier for mosquitos to multiply in the summer.

28. 利息 （ㄌㄧˋ ㄒㄧˊ；lishí）
    N：interest
    他一年利息的收入就有十萬美金。

His annual income from interest is one hundred thousand U.S. dollars.

29. 老本兒 (ㄌㄠˇ ㄅㄣˇ･ㄦ ; lǎuběnr)

    the original investment ; capital ; one's last stakes

II. 成　語

1. 殺雞取卵 (ㄕㄚ ㄐㄧ ㄑㄩˇ ㄌㄨㄢˇ ; shājīchiǔluǎn)

    to kill the hen that lays the golden eggs

2. 將本求利 (ㄐㄧㄤ ㄅㄣˇ ㄑㄧㄡˊ ㄌㄧˋ ; jiāngběnchióuli)

    (Lit.) with using capital to earn profit
    他做生意都是規規矩矩的將本求利，也著實賺了一筆錢。
    In doing business, he always honestly uses his capital to make profit. He certainly made some money.

III. 詞組與句型

1. 總覺得　always feel…

    你總覺得錢不夠花。
    You always feel there's not enough money to spend.
    我總覺得日子過得很慢。
    I always feel the days pass very slowly.

2. 雖然…，但　Although…,

    雖然他念了很多書，但是他不太懂做人的道理。
    Although he has studied a lot, yet he doesn't really understand the importance of dealing with others.

雖然他是個天才，但是他一點也不驕傲。
Although he's a genius, he's not proud at all.

3. 愛怎麼 v，就怎麼 v how what / ever you / want wish

你要怎麼做，就怎麼做。
Do it however you want.
你愛怎麼吃，就怎麼吃。
Eat whatever you wish.

4. 一…，就 as soon as

我一想到他就生氣。
As soon as I thought of him, I was angry.
我一看到他就知道他很聰明。
As soon as I saw him, I knew he was intelligent

IV. 練 習

1. 用下列詞語造句：

    1)有一對
    2)每天
    3)這是
    4)讓
    5)可以
    6)要想
    7)能夠
    8)怎麼
    9)還有

10)要是

2. 回答下列問題：

1)那對夫婦養了一隻什麼雞？
2)天帝爲什麼要給他們一隻會生金雞蛋的母雞呢？
3)他們的生活過得還好嗎？
4)這對老夫婦心裏想些什麼？
5)每天一個小金雞蛋夠不夠買很多的東西？
6)那些東西，他們沒法子買？
7)爲什麼？他們要把母雞給殺了？
8)母雞的肚子裏有很多金雞蛋嗎？
9)殺了母雞，每天還有固定的收入嗎？
10)爲什麼沒有了？

第二課　溫柔的月姊兒

　　從前有一對美麗的姊妹。姊姊溫柔嫻靜，妹妹艷麗剛烈。因為長得很漂亮，許多男孩子都藉故來親近她們。妹妹很討厭別人直瞪著眼睛看她。她說：「假使有人這樣看我，我就用繡花針，刺瞎他的眼睛。」姊姊勸她說：「有人這樣看妳，妳就躲開他吧！」但妹妹並不想聽從姊姊的話。

　　這一對姊妹就是天上的月亮和太陽。月亮老是在雲裏躲躲藏藏，卻更吸引人欣賞。太陽雖然也有許多人在天還沒有亮以前，就起來趕往高山，趕往海邊，苦苦等她出來，甚至事先搭乘大船，到海上去迎接她。大家只盼望能見她一面；但見到了，卻又不敢正眼多看她幾眼，總是怕被她撒下的繡花針刺痛了眼睛；所

14　中國寓言故事

以只能在黃昏，當她回家的時候，癡癡地遠望著她又美又紅的背影。

溫柔的女人，總是比較容易討人喜愛。

I. 生字與生詞

1. **溫柔的** (ㄨㄣ ㄖㄡˊ ˙ㄉㄜ；wēnróude)
   AT：gentle and soft
   她是一個溫柔的女孩。
   She's a gentle and soft girl.

2. **姊妹** (ㄐㄧㄝˇ ㄇㄟˋ；jiěmèi)
   N：sisters
   姊　N：elder sister
   妹　N：younger sister
   她是姊姊，我是妹妹。
   She's the older sister；I'm the younger sister.

3. **嫻靜** (ㄒㄧㄢˊ ㄐㄧㄥˋ；shiánjing)
   SV：refined and serene；quiet and refined (woman)

4. **艷麗** (ㄧㄢˋ ㄌㄧˋ；yànlì)
   SV：radiantly beautiful and gorgeous
   瑪莉長得十分艷麗
   Marie looks absolutely stunning.

5. **剛烈** (ㄍㄤ ㄌㄧㄝˋ；gānglie)
   SV：tough and vehement；violent strong and hot tempered
   烈　SV：violent (temper)

6. **藉故** (ㄐㄧㄝˋ ㄍㄨˋ；jiègù)
   VO：to use... as an excuse；to find an excuse for...

第二課　温柔的月姊兒　17

今晚約會，你不可藉故不來。
Don't find any excuse for not coming to date tonight.

7. 親近（ㄑㄧㄣ ㄐㄧㄣˋ；chīnjìn）

　　FV：to get close to
　　SV：be close to...；intimate
　　他和他的家人不很親近。
　　He's not very close to his family.

8. 討厭（ㄊㄠˇ ㄧㄢˋ；tǎuyàn）

　　FV：to dislike
　　To feel annoyed；irritated；to be weary of；to hate
　　SV： 1)disagreeable；disgusting；repugnant
　　　　　討厭的天氣。
　　　　　a intolerable weather
　　　　2)troublesome；hard to handle；nasty
　　　　　氣管炎是很討厭的病。
　　　　　Tracheitis is a nasty illness.
　　我最討厭下雨天。
　　I hate rainy days the most.
　　討　FV：to elicit；to ask for；to get；to incur
　　要討人喜歡不是件容易的事。
　　To gain someone's affection is not an easy thing.

9. 瞪著（ㄉㄥˋ·ㄓㄜ；dèngje）

　　FV：to stare at；to rivet one's gaze on...
　　請你不要一直瞪著我。
　　Please don't keep staring at me.

10. 假使（ㄐㄧㄚˇ ㄕˇ; jiǎshř）
    if; supposing
    假使我做錯了，請你告訴我。
    If I do it wrong, tell me, please.

11. 繡花針（ㄒㄧㄡˋ ㄏㄨㄚ ㄓㄣ; shiòuhuājēn）
    N：needle used to embroider
    繡花針是用來繡花的
    Embroidery needles are used for embroidering.

12. 勸（ㄑㄩㄢˋ; chiuàn）
    FV：to urge; to exhort; to caution; to advise
    我們勸他別去，他還是要去。
    We advised him not to go, but he still went.

13. 聽從（ㄊㄧㄥ ㄘㄨㄥˊ; tīngtsúng）
    FV：to obey; to listen to; be obedient to
    那個小孩子聽從母親的勸告，不再吃糖果。
    Heeding his mother's admonishment, that child never ate candy again.

14. 躲躲藏藏（ㄉㄨㄛˇ ㄉㄨㄛˇ ㄘㄤˊ ㄘㄤˊ; duǒduǒtsángtsáng）
    SV (AABB)：to hide; to avoid
    你爲什麼老是躲躲藏藏？欠人錢嗎？
    Why are you always avoiding people? Do you owe someone money?
    藏：FV：to hide; to conceal; to store; to hoard

第二課　溫柔的月姊兒　19

15. 吸引（ㄒㄧ ㄧㄣˇ；shīyǐn）
   FV：to attract；to entice
   她是一個很吸引人的女人。
   She's a very attractive lady.

16. 欣賞（ㄒㄧㄣ ㄕㄤˇ；shīnshǎng）
   FV：to appreciate；to admire；to enjoy
   大家都欣賞他認真工作的態度。
   Everyone appreciates his hard working attitude.

17. 趕（ㄍㄢˇ；gǎn）
   FV：to make a dash for；to pursue；to catch up；to hurry；to rush
   每天一大早，我就趕著去學校上課。
   Early every morning, I hurry off to school for class.

18. 事先（ㄕˋ ㄒㄧㄢ；shrshiān）
   A：prior to the event, at the outset
   我事先就有了準備。
   I was ready before it happened.

19. 搭乘（ㄉㄚ ㄔㄥˊ；dāchéng）
   FV：to ride in (a train, bus, airplane, etc.)
   她搭乘輪船去紐約。
   She's going to New York by boat.

20. 迎接（ㄧㄥˊ ㄐㄧㄝ；yíngjiē）
   FV：to welcome；to greet；to receive

我的叔叔從<u>巴黎</u>來，大家都去機場迎接他。
My uncle is coming from Paris. Everyone is going to the airport to welcome him.

21. 不敢（ㄅㄨˋ ㄍㄢˇ；bùgǎn）

　　AV：dare not
　　他到國外什麼都不敢吃，沒多久就瘦了一公斤。
　　He dare not eat anything abroad. Before long he had lost one kilogram.

22. 撒（ㄙㄚˇ；sǎ）

　　to scatter ; to sprinkle ; to disperse

23. 黃昏（ㄏㄨㄤˊ ㄏㄨㄣ；huánghuēn）

　　N：dusk, twilight
　　夕陽無限好，只是近黃昏。
　　The sunset is absolutely beautiful, but it's nearly twilight (from a Táng poem this Chinese proverb describes the ephemeral nature of beauty and life)

24. 癡癡地（ㄔ ㄔ ˙ㄉㄜ；chrchrde）

　　A：dazedly, in a mesmerized manner
　　那個少女癡癡地唱著：「何日君再來。」
　　In a daze, the young girl sang, "When Shalt Thou Return?"
　　癡　SV：be infatuated

II. 詞組與句型

1. 從前…

once upon a time ; in the past
從前他是一個很老實的人。
He was an honest man in the past.

2. 甚至

even ; even to the extent that...
他喜歡她,甚至愛她。
He likes her to the point of loving her.
她不但不幫忙,甚至在背後說他壞話。
Not only did she not help, she even spoke evil of him behind his back.

3. 當…的時候

when ; during
當她回到家的時候,…
when she gets home...
當我們勝利的時候,…
when we win...

4. 又…又

both... and
她又溫柔又美麗。
She is both gentle and beautiful.

III. 練 習

1. 用下列詞語造句：

   1)從前
   2)美麗
   3)長得
   4)假使
   5)就
   6)卻
   7)更
   8)甚至
   9)不敢
   10)回家

2. 回答下列問題：

   1)這一對姊妹，她們是怎麼樣的人？
   2)她們長得漂亮不漂亮？
   3)附近的男孩子喜歡不喜歡她們？
   4)妹妹喜歡人瞪著眼睛看她嗎？
   5)她用什麼方法對付他們呢？
   6)你知道，這兩個姊妹是誰呢？
   7)你喜歡月亮，還是喜歡太陽？
   8)要是你想看太陽，是到山上去看？還是到海邊去看？
   9)那些男人，為什麼不敢正眼看一看太陽呢？
   10)你說：那一種女孩子比較討人喜歡呢？

第三課　美姿巧舌

　　在北京城裏，有一個喜歡養鳥兒的有錢人。他從各地搜購了幾百種鳥，建造了一座鳥園，僱用一些懂得鳥語的人來管理飼養。他整日裏看鳥兒飛翔，聽鳥兒歌唱，十分快樂。

　　有一天，他聽說有一個商人從國外進口了一對珍禽，一隻舞姿優美，叫做「美姿」；一隻歌聲婉轉，叫做「巧舌」。於是這位有錢人就去拜訪那個商人，他見到了那對珍禽，非常喜歡，不惜重酬買了回來。

　　他把這兩隻鳥帶回鳥園後，特別用雕玉做鳥籠，又用香稻來飼養牠們。這兩隻鳥兒很會唱歌跳舞，美妙動人；大家都喜歡牠們。

　　過去，其他的鳥兒在沒有好手比較之下，亂跳亂唱，尚可博得大家的歡心。現在一比

— 23 —

24　中國寓言故事

較，顯得樣樣都不如新來的，自然不受人重視。可是牠們不知自己要努力求進步，卻反而大聲叫嚷，抱怨主人對牠們的待遇不公平。

　　管理鳥園的人勸告牠們說：「你們不要埋怨待遇低。其實，你們的才能很普通；今天的世界競爭很激烈，除了要有優異的才能外，還要能說悅耳好聽的話，還得有表演的天才，能做出一些討人歡心的姿態。美姿和巧舌，牠們所以能得到大家的喜歡，除了有能言善道的嘴巴和演技外，也還有些真實的本領的呢！」

I. 生字與生詞

1. **搜購** (ㄙㄡ ㄍㄡˋ; sōugòu)

   FV：to collect；select for purchase (a large amount of goods from many different sources, a rare item difficult to find, etc)
   他每到一個地方，就搜購當地的土產。
   Wherever he goes, he collects and buys the local products.
   搜　FV：to search
   購　FV：to buy；to purchase

2. **建造** (ㄐㄧㄢˋ ㄗㄠˋ; jiàntzàu)

   FV：to build；to construct
   附近建造了許多大樓。
   Many buildings have been constructed nearby.

3. **僱用** (ㄍㄨˋ ㄩㄥˋ; gùyùng)

   FV：to hire；to employ
   這家工廠僱用了不少工人。
   This factory employs many workers.

4. **管理** (ㄍㄨㄢˇ ㄌㄧˇ; guǎnlǐ)

   FV：to manage；to handle
   管理工廠是不容易的事。
   Managing a factory is not an easy thing to do.

5. **飼養** (ㄙˋ ㄧㄤˇ; szyǎng)

   FV：to raise；to breed

6. 飛翔（ㄈㄟ ㄒㄧㄤˊ；fēishiáng）
   FV：to fly；to hover

7. 珍禽（ㄓㄣ ㄑㄧㄣˊ；jēnchín）
   N：a rare bird
   珍　SV：precious；rare；very valuable

8. 舞姿（ㄨˇ ㄗ；wǔtz）
   N：a dancers postures and movements

9. 優美（ㄧㄡ ㄇㄟˇ；yōuměi）
   SV：graceful and elegant (visual)；equisite (auditory)
   那位婦人的姿態優美極了。
   That lady has an extremely elegant manner.

10. 婉囀（ㄨㄢˇ ㄓㄨㄢˇ；wǎnjuǎn）
    SV：a sweetvoice；very pleasing to the ear

11. 巧舌（ㄑㄧㄠˇ ㄕㄜˊ；chiǎushé）
    IE：eloquent；glib
    巧　SV：clever；ingenious；skillful
    A：coincidentally as it happens
    N：coincidence
    無巧不成書
    There is no story without coincidence.
    怎麼那麼巧！
    What a coincidence！
    巧妙　SV（ㄑㄧㄠˇ ㄇㄧㄠˋ；chiǎumiàu）

ingenious；skillful
這篇文章用字很巧妙。
The wording of this essay was skillful.

12. 不惜（ㄅㄨˋ ㄒㄧˊ；bùshí）

FV：at all cost；at any cost without regard to the price or consequences.
他們不惜任何代價，爭取自由。
Regardless of any cost, they strive for freedom.

13. 重酬（ㄓㄨㄥˋ ㄔㄡˊ；jùngchóu）

N：a substantial reward given in return for something；remuneration
他因爲撿到一隻小狗還給主人得到了一份重酬。
Because he found a puppy and returned it to its owner, he got a large reward.

14. 雕（ㄉㄧㄠ；diāu）

FV：to engrave

15. 籠（ㄌㄨㄥˊ；lúng）

N：a cage

16. 香稻（ㄒㄧㄤ ㄉㄠˋ；shiāngdàu）

N：rice (poetical)

17. 美妙（ㄇㄟˇ ㄇㄧㄠˋ；měimiàu）

SV：exquisite；very pleasant
她的歌聲非常美妙。

Her singing voice is really exquisite.

18. 動人 (ㄉㄨㄥˋ ㄖㄣˊ ; dùngrén)

    SV：moving (as in feelings, emotions)
    這是一個很動人的故事。
    This is a very moving story.

19. 好手 (ㄏㄠˇ ㄕㄡˇ ; hǎushǒu)

    IE：an expert (involving some kind of manual skill)；good hand；be adept at
    他是修車好手。
    He's an expert at fixing cars.

20. 尚可 (ㄕㄤˋ ㄎㄜˇ ; shàngkě)

    SV：passable；acceptable
    他的成績尚可。
    His grades are acceptable.

21. 博得 (ㄅㄛˊ ㄉㄜˊ ; bódé)

    FV：to obtain；to win

22. 歡心 (ㄏㄨㄢ ㄒㄧㄣ ; huānshīn)

    N：(to win another's) favour or heart
    他很用功唸書，所以得到老師的歡心。
    Because he studies very hard, he has won the teacher's favor.

23. 顯得 (ㄒㄧㄢˇ ㄉㄜˊ ; shiǎndé)

    RC：to look；to appear

他顯得非常愉快。
He looks very happy.

24. 樣樣（ㄧㄤˋ ㄧㄤˋ；yàngyàng）

PN：every sort；every variety；everything；each and every

我覺得自己樣樣都比不上別人。
I feel that in all aspects, I am inferior to others.

25. 不如（ㄅㄨˋ ㄖㄨˊ；bùrú）

FV：not as good as

我的文章不如你好。
My essay is not as good as yours.

26. 重視（ㄓㄨㄥˋ ㄕˋ；jùngshr̀）

FV：to consider important；to attach much importance to.

中國人很重視人情味。
The Chinese are attached great importance to friendliness and hospitality.

27. 進步（ㄐㄧㄣˋ ㄅㄨˋ；jìnbù）

N：improvement；progress；advancement

你的中文進步很多。
Your Chinese has improved a lot.

FV：advance；improve

AT：progressive

28. 叫嚷（ㄐㄧㄠˋ ㄖㄤˇ；jiàurǎng）

FV：shout, make a great noise

29. 抱怨（ㄅㄠˋ ㄩㄢˋ；bàuyuàn）

FV：to complain；to grumble
我討厭他常常抱怨。
I am sick of him complaining so often.

30. 待遇（ㄉㄞˋ ㄩˋ；dàiyù）

N：pay；salary；treatment
老師應該給予學生同等待遇。
A teacher should give every student equal treatment.
待　（ㄉㄞˋ；dài）
FV：to treat；to entertain；to wait
遇　（ㄩˋ；yù）
N & FV：to treatment；to meet；to come across

31. 競爭（ㄐㄧㄥˋ ㄓㄥ；jìngjēng）

N：competition
FV：to compete.

32. 激烈（ㄐㄧ ㄌㄧㄝˋ；jīliè）

SV：heated (debate, battle, etc)；drastic (measures, means, etc)；violent (actions, speeches, etc)；radical (party, etc)
商場競爭很激烈。
Competition in the market place is fierce.

33. 優異（ㄧㄡ ㄧˋ；yōuyì）

SV：outstanding；remarkable
他是班上最優異的學生。
He is the most outstanding student in the class.

34. 表演（ㄅㄧㄠˇ ㄧㄢˇ；biǎuyǎn）

FV & N：to perform；performance
他有表演的天分。
He is a born actor.
演　FV：to act；to perform；to expound；to exercise
她曾上台演過戲嗎？
Did she ever act on the stage?

35. 天才（ㄊㄧㄢ ㄘㄞˊ；tiāntsái）

N：a genius；genius
他是數學的天才。
He is a genius at Mathematics.

36. 姿態（ㄗ ㄊㄞˋ；tztài）

N：poise；bearing；carriage；manner
她有優美的姿態。
She has a fine poise.

37. 演技（ㄧㄢˇ ㄐㄧˋ；yǎnjì）

N：acting skill
她演技精湛。
She has good acting skill.
技　N：special ability；skill；ingenuity；dexterity

38. 本領（ㄅㄣˇ ㄌㄧㄥˇ；běnlǐng）

N：talent；ability；skill
他一點真實的本領都沒有。
He has no real abilities whatsoever.

II. 成語

1. 美姿巧舌（ㄇㄟˇ ㄗ ㄑㄧㄠˇ ㄕㄜˊ；měitzchiǎushé）
   beautiful in poise and bearing, and eloquent in speech

2. 如簧之舌（ㄖㄨˊ ㄏㄨㄤˊ ㄓ ㄕㄜˊ；rúhuángjrshé）
   eloquent; a glib tongue
   鼓動如簧之舌
   Rouse the tongue like playing a real-organ; way one's tongue

3. 悅耳好聽（ㄩㄝˋ ㄦˇ ㄏㄠˇ ㄊㄧㄥ；yueěrhǎutīng）
   pleasing to the ear; sweet sounding
   她的歌聲「悅耳好聽」，因此大家都喜歡她唱歌。
   Because her singing is pleasant, everbody likes to hear her sing.

4. 能言善道（ㄋㄥˊ ㄧㄢˊ ㄕㄢˋ ㄉㄠˋ；néngyánshàndàu）
   eloquent; have the gift of the gab; have a glib tongue
   (Lit.) able to speak and know how to say it properly; have a ready tongue
   他是一個能言善道的人。
   He is an eloquent person.

5. 敢做敢為（ㄍㄢˇ ㄗㄨㄛˋ ㄍㄢˇ ㄨㄟˊ；gǎntzuògǎnwéi）
   (Lit) venture to do and dare to act; take one's courage in both hands

羅賓漢是一個敢做敢為的人物。
Robin Hood was a person who had the courage to do what he believed in.

III. 詞組與句型

1. 用…來

to use... to ; to use... for ; to use... as
他用腳踏車來做交通工具。
He uses a bicycle as his means of transport.
我用自己賺的錢來完成學業。
I use the money I have made to complete my studies.

2. 在…之下

under, from
在他照顧之下，我的病漸漸好了起來。
Under his care, my sickness gradually got better.
在你的教導之下，我的中文愈來愈進步了。
Under your instruction, my Chinese is getting better and better.

3. 除了…以外，還得（有）…

besides (as well as)..., ... must also have
除了有好的頭腦以外，還得有健康的身體。
As well as brains, you must also have a healthy body.
學中文除了要有好的老師以外，還得自己多多用功。
To study Chinese, besides (needing) a good teacher, you must also study hard.

IV. 練　習

1. 用下列詞語造句：

    1) 搜購
    2) 建造
    3) 僱用
    4) 管理
    5) 進口
    6) 叫做
    7) 抱怨
    8) 競爭
    9) 表演
    10) 本領

2. 回答下列問題：

    1) 那個有錢人喜歡養那些小動物？
    2) 他養鳥做什麼？
    3) 商人從外國進口了兩隻甚麼樣的小鳥？
    4) 他有沒有買到這兩隻珍奇的小鳥？
    5) 大家為什麼都喜歡這兩隻新來的小鳥呢？
    6) 其他的鳥抱怨待遇不公平，有沒有道理？
    7) 今天，人與人之間的競爭激烈嗎？
    8) 你認為一個人需要不需要具有優秀的才能？
    9) 你是個能言善道的人嗎？
    10) 你有沒有真實的本領？

第四課　點石成金

　　從前，有一個神仙，有「點石成金」的本領。他只要用食指一指，砂粒就會變成光彩耀眼的金子，石頭也會變成人見人愛的金塊。他想用點石成金的法術來試探人心，打算在這個世界上，找一個最不貪心的人，度化他成為長生不老的神仙。他找了好幾年，也沒找到一個人。他就是將大石頭變成金子給人；那些人都還嫌小呢！

　　有一天，這個神仙遇到一個人；他用手指頭指著一個小石頭，喝一聲「變」，就把這個小石頭變成了黃澄澄的金子，說：「我把這塊金子送給你；你要不要？」那個人搖搖頭，表示不要。

　　神仙以為他嫌那塊金子不夠大，又指著一

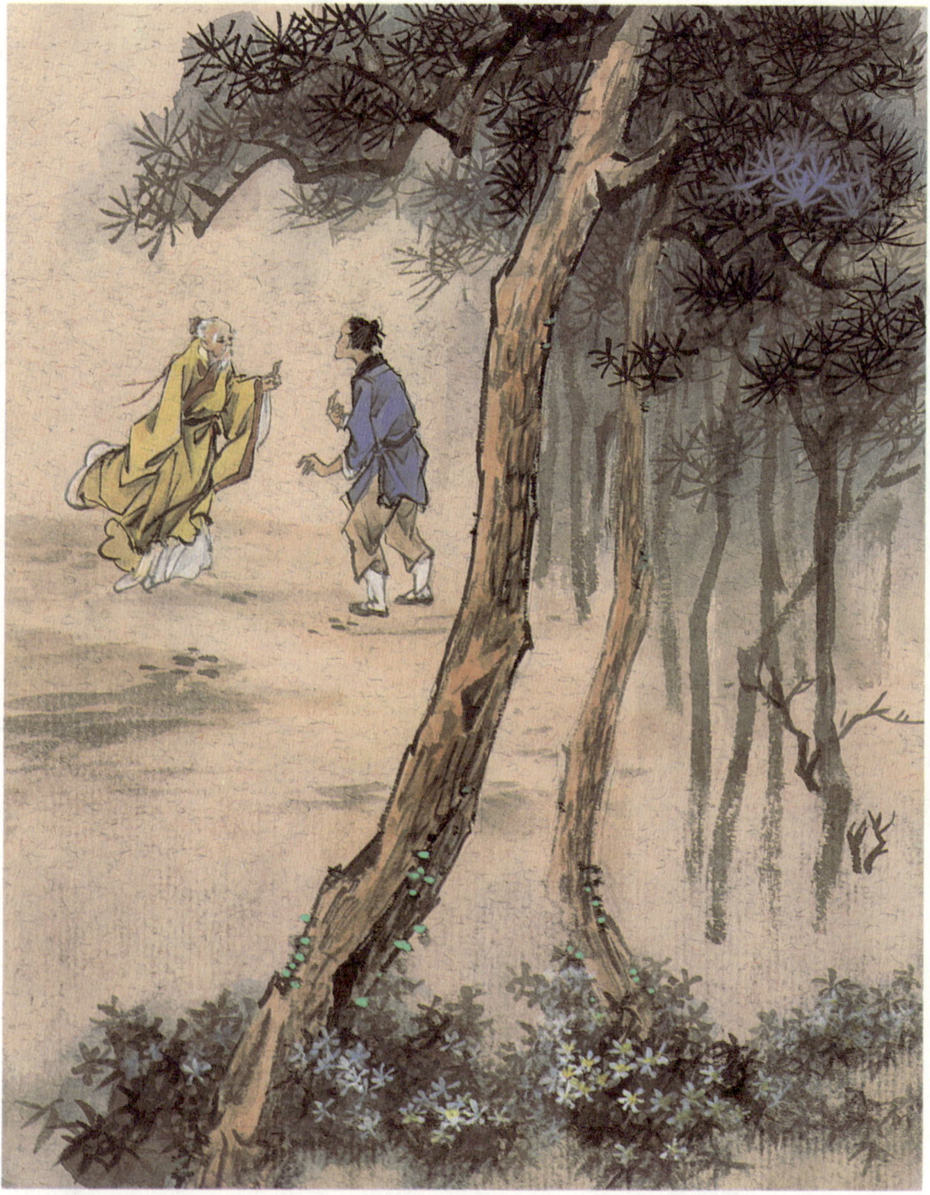

塊更大的石頭，說：「那我把這塊大石頭，變成金子給你吧！」說著，又用手指一點，果然又變成了黃金。

那個人還是搖頭不要。

神仙心想這個人，沒有一點兒貪心，實在很難得，我應該讓他變成神仙，才說：「大小金子，你都不要。那你要什麼？」

那個人伸出食指來說：「別的，我都不要。我只要你把那個能夠『點石成金』的食指，換到我的手上就好了！那樣，我就可以隨意點石成金，不用麻煩你了。」

世人沒有不愛錢的，所以直到今天，還沒有一個「凡人」變成神仙！

Ⅰ. 生字與生詞

1. 神仙（ㄕㄣˊ ㄒㄧㄢ；shénshiān）

   N：celestial being
   a supernatural being；an immortal；a fairy
   有些人相信世界上有神仙存在。
   Some people believe in the existence of immortals in the world.

2. 食指（ㄕˊ ㄓˇ；shŕjǐ）

   N：index finger

3. 砂粒（ㄕㄚ ㄌㄧˋ；shālì）

   N：sand；grit
   砂　N：sand；gravel
   粒　M：a grain (measure word for rice, sand, etc)；a pill；a bead

4. 光彩（ㄍㄨㄤ ㄘㄞˇ；guāngtsǎi）

   N & SV：luster；sheen；gloss

5. 耀眼（ㄧㄠˋ ㄧㄢˇ；yàuyǎn）

   SV：dazzling
   這是一顆很耀眼的寶石。
   This is a very dazzling gem.

6. 法術（ㄈㄚˇ ㄕㄨˋ；fǎshù）

   N：an uncanny, occult, or supernatural feat；magic skills

神仙有飛行天空，不吃食物，長生不老等法術。
An immortal has every kind of magic skill to flying through space, not eating anything, and staying young forever.

7. 試探（ㄕˋ ㄊㄢˋ；shr̀tàn）

    FV：to test；to fathom；to sound out
    女人喜歡試探男人，看他是不是愛她。
    Women like to test men to see if they love them.

8. 貪心（ㄊㄢ ㄒㄧㄣ；tānshīn）

    SV：greedy
    我不是個貪心的人。
    I'm not a greedy person.

9. 度化（ㄉㄨˋ ㄏㄨㄚˋ；dùhuà）

    FV：to deliver (someone) to a higher realm

10. 嫌（ㄒㄧㄢˊ；shián）

    FV：to be unsatisfied with (something)
    我給你兩千塊，你還嫌少。
    I gave you two thousand dollars and you still think it's too small a sum.

11. 遇到（ㄩˋ ㄉㄠˋ；yùdàu）

    FV：to meet；to encounter
    我們在街上遇到她。
    We met her in the street.

12. 黃澄澄的（ㄏㄨㄤˊ ㄔㄥˊ ㄔㄥˊ ˙ㄉㄜ；

huángchéngchéngde）

AT：golden yellow

13. 搖搖頭（ㄧㄠˊ ㄧㄠˊ ㄊㄡˊ；yáuyáutóu）

VO：to shake the head (for a negative reply or out of sympathy)

我爸爸只對我搖搖頭，什麼也沒說。

My father only shook his head at me, saying nothing.

14. 表示（ㄅㄧㄠˇ ㄕˋ；biǎushr̀）

FV：to indicate；to show

他不敢對她表示他的愛。

He doesn't dare express his love to her.

15. 以為（ㄧˇ ㄨㄟˊ；yǐwéi）

FV：to regard, to think, to consider
to mistake…for…

我以為她是你的太太，今天才知道她是你的妹妹。

I mistake her for your wife. It's only today I found out she is your younger sister.

16. 果然（ㄍㄨㄛˇ ㄖㄢˊ；guǒrán）

MA：as expected；exactly as one expected

今天的天氣果然和我想的一樣。

As expected, today's weather is like I thought it would be.

17. 難得（ㄋㄢˊ ㄉㄜˊ；nándé）

SV：rare；hard to come by

A：seldom；rarely
這是一次難得的經驗
This is a rare experience.

18. 伸出（ㄕㄣ ㄔㄨ；shēnchū）

DV：to extend；to stretch out
母親伸出兩手，把那個孩子擁在懷裡。
The mother extended her arms and embraced the child in her bosom.

19. 隨意（ㄙㄨㄟˊ ㄧˋ；suéiyì）

A：according to your wish；as you like it；to act as one pleases
你可以隨意寫你喜歡的東西。
You may write about anything as you please.

20. 麻煩（ㄇㄚˊ ㄈㄢˊ；máfán）

FV：trouble；troublesome
麻煩你幫我查一下。
Could you please help me check it.
SV：這件事很麻煩。
This is a troublesome thing.

21. 凡人（ㄈㄢˊ ㄖㄣˊ；fánrén）

N：an ordinary person；one of the masses；a mortal
他只是一個凡人，不是神仙，聖人，英雄，平凡地過了一生。
He's not an immortal, a saint or a hero. He's just an ordinary guy, living an ordinary life.

II. 成語

1. **點石成金**（ㄉㄧㄢˇ ㄕˊ ㄔㄥˊ ㄐㄧㄣ；diǎnshŕchéngjīn）
   (Lit) Touch a stone and turn it into gold
   不要夢想你可以點石成金。
   Don't dream you can turn stone into gold all the time.

2. **人見人愛**（ㄖㄣˊ ㄐㄧㄢˋ ㄖㄣˊ ㄞˋ；rénjiànrén-ài）
   whoever see him(it) will like him(it)；likeable
   他是一個人見人愛的孩子，非常天真活潑。
   He is a likeable child, very innocent and lively.

3. **長生不老**（ㄔㄤˊ ㄕㄥ ㄅㄨˋ ㄌㄠˇ；chángshēngbùlǎo）
   immortality and eternal youth.
   每個人都想要長生不老。
   Everybody wants immortality and eternal youth.

III. 詞組與句型

1. **只要…就會**
   only need to…, then…will；if…, then…will；as long as…, …will
   你只要天天運動，身體就會健康。
   As long as you exercise everyday, your body will be in good shape.

IV. 練　習

1. 用下列詞語造句：

    1) 神仙
    2) 金子
    3) 變成
    4) 打算
    5) 嫌
    6) 要
    7) 給
    8) 讓
    9) 換
    10) 隨意

2. 回答下列問題：

    1) 這位神仙有什麼本領？
    2) 金子，大家都喜歡嗎？
    3) 你也喜歡金子嗎？
    4) 那個人卻為什麼不喜歡神仙給他的金塊？
    5) 他到底想要什麼？
    6) 這樣看來，他也是一個貪心的人了？
    7) 貪心的人能不能夠成為神仙？
    8) 黃金真從石頭變來的嗎？
    9) 這篇故事是說：沒有人不貪心。你同意這種說法嗎？
    10) 請將理由說出？為什麼同意？為什麼不同意？

第五課　不要隨便跟人開玩笑

劉貢父很喜歡隨便跟朋友開玩笑。

有一天，蘇東坡對劉貢父說：「我和舍弟在外求學的時候，常常讀書入迷，忘了弄飯，就吃些『三白』；吃過了三白，你就不相信世間還有更好吃的東西了。」

劉貢父問：「什麼是『三白』？」

東坡說：「一撮雪白的鹽，一碟嫩白的生蘿蔔，一碗香甜的白米飯，就是『三白』。」

劉貢父聽了大笑。

過了幾個月，有一天，劉貢父忽然下帖子請東坡吃「皛」飯。東坡看了請帖，對人說：「貢父讀書很多，這個『皛飯』一定很特別。」

蘇東坡到了劉貢父的家裡，看到一張大飯

48　中國寓言故事

桌上只擺著白鹽、白蘿蔔和白飯三樣,這才領悟到——原來是劉貢父用他說過「三白」的話,跟他開開玩笑罷了。他只好坐下,高高興興地把它吃完。他吃過飯,告辭出門,將要上馬時候,回過頭來,對劉貢父說:「明天中午,讓我回請你。我一回去,就去準備『毳飯』大餐,務請賞光。」劉貢父雖然害怕東坡戲弄自己,但不知道「毳飯」是什麼好吃的佳肴。

　　劉貢父如期前往蘇家。東坡非常殷勤地招待他,和他喝茶聊天,空腹灌了一肚子的茶水,談了好半天的閒話,看看時間已經過了中午好久,主人家還沒有把飯菜端上桌來。到了下午兩點多鐘,肚子餓得難受極了,就跟東坡說:「什麼好吃的菜,快一點端上來吧!」東坡說:「再等一會兒吧。」

　　這樣又過了好一陣子。貢父又叫:「東坡兄,我的肚子餓極了。菜不必做的太精緻,叫

廚子隨便先來一點兒吃的吧！」東坡答應如舊。又過了一下子，貢父又說：「怎麼還不上飯呢！我已經餓到不能再忍受了。」

東坡說：「鹽也毛，蘿蔔也毛，飯也毛，不是『三毛飯』嗎？」

這個故事就是告訴我們，就算非常要好的朋友，也不可以隨便跟他開玩笑。從這個故事，還可以知道中國的文字是很有趣味的，有些字可以拆開，也可以拼合來用；像三個「白」字拼合起來，就成了「皛」字。有些字讀音相同，又可以借用像「毛」字和「没」字同音，就借「毛」字做「没」字；所以「毳飯」就是白鹽、白蘿蔔和白飯三樣都沒有的意思。

第五課　不要隨便跟人開玩笑　51

Ⅰ. 生字與生詞

1. 劉貢父（ㄌㄧㄡˊ ㄍㄨㄥˋ ㄈㄨˇ；lióugùngfǔ）
   N：Lióu Gùng-fǔ (A.D. 1022-1088)
   A good friend of Sū Dūng-pō.

2. 蘇東坡（ㄙㄨ ㄉㄨㄥ ㄆㄛ；sūdūngpō）
   N：Sū Dūng-pō (A.D. 1036-1101), Statesman (rising to the position of Minister of rites and education), scholar and artist. His poems, essays, lyrics, calligraphy and silk paintings were all very famous.

3. 舍弟（ㄕㄜˋ ㄉㄧˋ；shèdì）
   N：my younger brother
   最近，舍弟去了美國。
   My brother went to the United States recently.

4. 入迷（ㄖㄨˋ ㄇㄧˊ；rùmí）
   SV：to be captivated by or be bewitched；be facinated；be engrossed in；be enhanced
   看電視不要看得太入迷了。
   Don't watch T.V. to the point of being captivated.
   他讀書入迷。
   He was captivated by reading books.
   他被她的美麗迷住了。
   He was a captive to her beauty.

5. 一撮（ㄧ ㄘㄨㄛˋ；yìtsuò）

M：a pinch
一撮鹽
a pinch of salt

6. 雪白（ㄒㄩㄝˋ ㄅㄞˊ；shiuèbái）

SV：snow-white；snowy
那個女孩子有非常美的雪白皮膚。
That girl has very beautiful, snow-white skin.
這老太婆有雪白的頭髮。
The old lady has snowy hair.

7. 鹽（ㄧㄢˊ；yán）

N：salt
請給我一撮鹽。
Please give me a pinch of salt.

8. 碟（ㄉㄧㄝˊ；dié）

N & M：a small plate

9. 生（ㄕㄥ；shēng）

SV：raw；uncooked
沙拉是用生菜做的。
Salad is made from raw vegetables.
我喜歡吃生菜和生魚片。
I like to eat salad and raw fish.

10. 蘿蔔（ㄌㄨㄛˊ·ㄅㄛ；luóbo）

N：a radish
紅蘿蔔（a carrot）

11. 一碗（ㄧˋ ㄨㄢˇ；yìwǎn）

N & M：a bowl of
小姐，請再來一碗飯。
Waitress, please bring another bowl of rice.

12. 下帖子（ㄒㄧㄚˋ ㄊㄧㄝˇ・ㄗ；shiàtiětz）

VO：to give an invitation
你結婚的時候，別忘了下帖子給我。
When you get married, don't forget to give me an invitation.

13. 擺（ㄅㄞˇ；bǎi）

FV：to arrange；to display；to place；to be arranged, placed, etc.
飯桌上擺著許多食物。
There's a lot of food laid out on the dining table.

14. 領悟（ㄌㄧㄥˇ ㄨˋ；lǐngwù）

FV：to comprehend；to understand；to realize
必須靠自己去領悟一些書中的道理。
One must rely on oneself to comprehend some significant meanings in books.

15. 罷了（ㄅㄚˋ・ㄌㄜ；bàle）

P：merely；only
我只是跟你開玩笑罷了。
I'm only joking with you.
這只是跟他開開玩笑罷了。

It is merely to play a jok with him.

16. 告辭（ㄍㄠˋ ㄘˊ; gàutsź）

    FV：to take leave ; to say good-bye (formal)
    我們必須告辭了。
    We must say goodbye.

17. 準備（ㄓㄨㄣˇ ㄅㄟˋ; juěnbèi）

    FV：to prepare ; to get ready ; to be prepared, etc.
    晚餐準備好了沒？
    Is dinner ready?

18. 務請（ㄨˋ ㄑㄧㄥˇ; wùchǐng）

    A：please be sure to
    務請把所有的事情都告訴我。
    Please be sure to tell me all the things.

19. 賞光（ㄕㄤˇ ㄍㄨㄤ; shǎngguāng）

    IE：to honour me (someone or some place) with your presence (formal) or company
    下禮拜我結婚，請你務必要賞光。
    I'm getting married next week. Please, you must honour us with your presence.

20. 戲弄（ㄒㄧˋ ㄋㄨㄥˋ; shì-nùng）

    FV：to play a practical joke on ; to make fun of
    別戲弄我了！
    Don't play jokes on me!

21. 佳肴（ㄐㄧㄚ ㄧㄠˊ；jiāyáu）
   N：excellent food or dishes
   供應極佳的菜肴
   to serve an excellent dishes.

22. 如期（ㄖㄨˊ ㄑㄧˊ；rúchí）
   A：punctually；at the appointed time

23. 前往（ㄑㄧㄢˊ ㄨㄤˇ；chiánwǎng）
   FV：to visit；to go to (a place)
   他們不知要前往何處去。
   They don't know where they want to go.

24. 殷勤（ㄧㄣ ㄑㄧㄣˊ；yīnchín）
   SV & A：courteous(ly)
   他待人非常殷勤。
   He treats people very courteously.

25. 招待（ㄓㄠ ㄉㄞˋ；jāudài）
   FV：to receive；to welcome；to look after (a guest)
   真對不起，菜不好，沒有好好招待你。
   Our apologies. The food is not good and we have not looked after you well.

26. 聊天（ㄌㄧㄠˊ ㄊㄧㄢ；liáutiān）
   FV：to chat with
   我和朋友聊天。
   I chatted with my friends.

N：Let's have a chat

27. 空腹（ㄎㄨㄥ ㄈㄨˋ；kūng fù）
an empty stomach

28. 灌（ㄍㄨㄢˋ；guàn）
to pour；to fill

29. 一肚子（ㄧ ㄉㄨˋ•ㄗ；yīdùtz）
M：a stomachful；a lot of…；full of…
他灌了一肚子的茶水。
His stomach is full of tea.
IE：她生了一肚子氣。
She is very angry.

30. 閒話（ㄒㄧㄢˊ ㄏㄨㄚˋ；shiánhuà）
N：idle talk

31. 端（ㄉㄨㄢ；duān）
FV：(to hold something. level with both hands)
請你把菜端上桌。
Please carry the food to the table.

32. 精緻（ㄐㄧㄥ ㄓˋ；jīngjr）
SV：exquisite

33. 廚子（ㄔㄨˊ•ㄗ；chútz）
N：a cook
他的太太是個好廚子。

His wife is a good cook.

34. 答應 (ㄉㄚ ㄧㄥˋ ; dāying)

FV：to promise ; to assent to (a request)
請你答應我的要求。
Please assent to my request.

35. 舊 (ㄐㄧㄡˋ ; jiòu)

SV：former ; old ; ancient
我喜歡穿舊衣服。
I like to wear old clothes.

36. 忍受 (ㄖㄣˇ ㄕㄡˋ ; rěnshòu)

FV to endure ; to bear
我無法忍受台北的交通。
I just can not endure Taipei traffic.

37. 毛 (ㄇㄛˋ ; mò)

A：In ancient China 「毛」 and 「沒」, both pronounced (ㄇㄛˋ ; mò), meant 沒有。

38. 拆開 (ㄔㄞ ㄎㄞ ; chāikāi)

RE：to separate ; to take apart ; to open (a letter, box, etc.)
組合家具可以拆開來用。
Combination furniture can be taken apart and used separately.

39. 拼合 (ㄆㄧㄣ ㄏㄜˊ ; pīnhé)

RE：to join together；to put together; to make a whole
他把拼圖拼合好了。
He put together the jigsaw puzzle.

40. 相同（ㄒㄧㄤ ㄊㄨㄥˊ；shiāngtúng）

SV：same；similar
中國字有很多讀音相同的字。
There are many Chinese characters that have the same pronunciation.

41. 借用（ㄐㄧㄝˋ ㄩㄥˋ；jièyùng）

FV：to borrow
我可以借用你的雨傘嗎？
Can I borrow your umbrella?

II. 成　語

1. 高高興興（ㄍㄠ ㄍㄠ ㄒㄧㄥˋ ㄒㄧㄥˋ；gāugāushìngshìng）

(Lit) Highly elated and delighted
他高高興興地唱歌。
He is singing happily.

III. 詞組與句型

1. 這⋯一定　　The (This)⋯must⋯

這個東西一定很特別。
This thing must be very special.
這本書一定很有內容。

The content of this book must be very good.
這個人看來一定很老實。
This person must be very honest looking.

2. 一…就　Once…

我一回去，就去準備晚飯。
Once I go back, I will prepare dinner.
他一來，討論就熱烈起來。
Once he came, the discussion became very exciting.
戰爭一爆發，就會造成重大的傷亡。
Once the war begins, there will be casualties.

IV. 練　習

1. 用下列詞語造句：

    1) 跟
    2) 入迷
    3) 擺著
    4) 吃過
    5) 準備
    6) 招待
    7) 端
    8) 上
    9) 趣味
    10) 借用

2. 回答下列問題：

 1) <u>蘇東坡</u>曾經跟<u>劉貢父</u>說過什麼事情？
 2) 什麼是三白？
 3) <u>劉貢父</u>請<u>蘇東坡</u>吃什麼飯？
 4) 「皛飯」是怎麼樣的一種特別的飯呢？
 5) <u>蘇東坡</u>回請<u>劉貢父</u>的「毳飯」，是好吃的大餐嗎？
 6) <u>蘇東坡</u>怎樣招待<u>劉貢父</u>？
 7) <u>劉貢父</u>以為「毳飯」是怎麼的一種飯？
 8) <u>蘇東坡</u>所準備的「毳飯」，到底是怎麼樣的一種飯呢？
 9) 這個故事的含意是什麼？
 10) 你讀了這個故事，能夠指出<u>中國</u>文字的特性嗎？

第六課　狡兔三窟

　　這是個晴朗的早晨，一隻小白兔在那片綠綠的山坡上，無憂無慮，逍遙自在地蹦蹦跳跳。

　　就在這個時候，忽然來了一隻灰色的野狼，咧開嘴巴，露著牙齒，流著口水，追著要吃小白兔。小白兔急急逃跑，狼卻緊追不捨。

　　小白兔被追得急了，跑到樹下，向猴子求救。猴子說：「快爬！快爬上樹來躲一躲！」小白兔不會爬樹，又急急忙忙地逃走，跑到了水邊，向青蛙求救。青蛙叫：「快跳！快跳下水來避一避！」小白兔不會游泳，又急急忙忙地離開，心裡想道：「求人不如求己。別人的辦法，自己用不上；還不如自己想個好辦法，來得切實。」牠一下子想通了，就急急忙忙跑

62　中國寓言故事

向山中，在樹叢下，挖了好幾個地道和小洞，又造了幾個出口。

從此再遇到大野狼，小白兔就由地道躲進山窟裡。因為地道入口小，貪婪的狼是沒法跟進去的；小白兔也就不怕野狼了。

猴子和青蛙都很佩服小白兔的智慧。後來連聰明的人類也都佩服兔子的智慧，向牠學習。

Ⅰ. 生字與生詞

1. 兔（ㄊㄨˋ；tù）
   N：a hare；a rabbit

2. 野狼（ㄧㄝˇ ㄌㄤˊ；yělángˊ）
   N：wolf

3. 咧開（ㄌㄧㄝˇ ㄎㄞ；liěkāi）
   RE：to open the mouth wide
   他咧開嘴巴大哭。
   He is crying with his mouth wide open。

4. 露（ㄌㄡˋ；lòu）
   FV：to reveal；to emerge；to show
   他媽媽常露出寂寞的表情。
   His mother often shows a lonely expression.

5. 牙齒（ㄧㄚˊ ㄔˇ；yáchˇ）
   N：the teeth；a tooth

6. 追（ㄓㄨㄟ；juēi）
   FV：to chase；to pursue；to follow
   警察追了十哩之後，才抓到了小偷。
   After chasing for 10 miles, the police caught the thief.

7. 猴子（ㄏㄡˊ ˙ㄗ；hóutz）
   N：a monkey

8. 求救（ㄑㄧㄡˊ ㄐㄧㄡˋ；chióujiòu）

    VO：to seek relief, to ask for rescue or help
    爸，我沒有錢了，只好向您求救了。
    Dad, I don't have any money, so I'm asking you for help.

9. 青蛙（ㄑㄧㄥ ㄨㄚ；chīngwā）

    N：a frog

10. 避（ㄅㄧˋ；bì）

    FV：to avoid；to evade；to hide

11. 切實（ㄑㄧㄝˋ ㄕˊ；chièshŕ）

    SV：sure；certain；thorough
    每天做白日夢還不如腳踏實地活著來得切實。
    Day dreaming everyday is not as certain and thorough as living with your feet firmly on the ground.

12. 想通了（ㄒㄧㄤˇ ㄊㄨㄥ ˙ㄌㄜ；shiǎngtūngle）

    RE：to have found the answer to a problem；to have figured it out
    你想通了沒有？
    Have you figured it out?

13. 樹叢（ㄕㄨˋ ㄘㄨㄥˊ；shùtsúng）

    N：a grove of trees

14. 地道（ㄉㄧˋ ㄉㄠˋ；dìdàu）

    N：a tunnel

古代的城堡，常常有地道，直通城外。
Forts in ancient times often had tunnels leading to the outskirts.

15. 小洞（ㄒㄧㄠˇ ㄉㄨㄥˋ；shiǎudùng）
    N：a small hole or cave

16. 窟（ㄎㄨ；kū）
    N：a hole；a cave；a pit；a den

17. 貪婪（ㄊㄢ ㄌㄢˊ；tānlán）
    SV：greed；covetousness

18. 智慧（ㄓˋ ㄏㄨㄟˋ；jrhuèi）
    N：intelligence；wisdom
    他是個充滿智慧的人。
    He is a person full of wisdom

II. 成　語

1. 狡兔三窟（ㄐㄧㄠˇ ㄊㄨˋ ㄙㄢ ㄎㄨ；jiǎutùsānkū）
   (Lit.) A cunning rabbit has three exits (as its burrow).
   「狡兔三窟」是個非常聰明的逃生辦法。
   "A wily rabbit has three burrows" is an extremely intelligent way of escape.

2. 蹦蹦跳跳（ㄅㄥˋ ㄅㄥˋ ㄊㄧㄠˋ ㄊㄧㄠˋ；bèngbèngtiàutiàu）
   Skipping；romping；jumping；frolicing
   不要在我面前蹦蹦跳跳。

Don't jump around in front of me.

3. 無憂無慮（ㄨˊ ㄧㄡ ㄨˊ ㄌㄩˋ；wúyōuwúlìu）

　　carefree；without a worry or care in the world
　　能夠無憂無慮地生活，就是最幸福的人。
　　A person who can live without a worry or a care is the most fortunate of all.

4. 逍遙自在（ㄒㄧㄠ ㄧㄠˊ ㄗˋ ㄗㄞˋ；shiāuyáutztzài）

　　(Lit) to wander about freely and happily
　　蝴蝶總是逍遙自在地飛舞著。
　　Butterflies always flutter about without a care.

5. 求人不如求己（ㄑㄧㄡˊ ㄖㄣˊ ㄅㄨˋ ㄖㄨˊ ㄑㄧㄡˊ ㄐㄧˇ；chióurén bùrú chióujǐ）

　　(Lit) asking others for help is not as good as asking oneself
　　求人不如求己，只要自己肯努力，任何困難都能解決。
　　Relying on yourself is better than relying on others；as long as you yourself are willing to work hard, then any difficulty can be solved.

III. 練　習

1. 用下列詞語造句：

　　1) 晴朗的
　　2) 綠綠的
　　3) 灰色的

4) 別人的
5) 貪婪的
6) 聰明的
7) 不會
8) 不如
9) 不怕
10) 用不上

2. 回答下列問題：

1) 小白兔最愛吃什麼東西？
2) 小白兔的生活快樂嗎？
3) 野狼要吃小白兔嗎？
4) 小白兔被野狼追急了，向誰求救？
5) 後來，小白兔又向誰求救？
6) 小白兔會爬樹嗎？會游水嗎？
7) 猴子和青蛙給小白兔想的辦法，有用嗎？
8) 後來小白兔怎麼辦，才躲過野狼的追逐？
9) 你能簡單地說出小白兔的「三窟」狡計的內容嗎？
10) 小白兔是不是也很有智慧？爲什麼？

第七課　攆驢進城

有一家住在鄉下的父子倆帶著一頭驢子進城。

起先，父親一個人騎在驢背上，兒子在後面跟著走。路上的行人說：「怎麼，這個老的自己舒舒服服地騎著驢，卻讓那小的辛辛苦苦地跟著跑，太不知道疼愛孩子了！」這個做父親的聽了就趕緊下來，讓兒子騎上驢背去，自己走路。

沒走多久，又有人說：「這個做孩子的真不像話，怎麼可以讓老爹走路，自己騎驢呢？」兒子聽了趕緊下來，陪他父親一起吆喝，趕著驢子走。

不多久，又有人笑著說：「啊哈！竟有這樣的人，放著牲口不騎，還要費那麼大勁兒，

70　中國寓言故事

吆喝著驢走路呢！再沒有比這更笨了！」跟在驢子後邊走，又惹人笑，也不是辦法。父子倆一商量，就乾脆兩個人一起騎上驢背上去了，壓得這頭驢子唔唔直叫，用力曲著背，走得十分吃力。

這時，又有人罵他們：「虐待動物。」說得這父子倆手足無措，真不知道該怎麼做才好！後來只好把這匹驢倒綁在一根粗木棍子上，父子一前一後，扛在肩膀上，擡進城裡去了。

這個擡驢進城的故事，似乎荒謬無稽，但細加品嚼，在我們的世界上，卻有很多這一類的事情，許多人常常耳朵軟，人說東就向東，人說西就向西；因此，原來非常妥當的措施，也常常因為聽多了不同的意見，反而不知道怎麼辦了，甚至處理失當，擱置不做的也有。

I. 生字與生詞

1. **抬**（ㄊㄞˊ；tái）

   FV：to lift；to raise.
   這箱子太重，我們抬不動。
   This box is too heavy for us to lift.

2. **驢**（ㄌㄩˊ；liú）

   N：a donkey

3. **倆**（ㄌㄧㄤˇ；liǎng）

   N：two people
   他兄弟倆都是工程師。
   Both the brothers are engineers.

4. **起先**（ㄑㄧˇ ㄒㄧㄢ；chǐshiān）

   A：in the beginning；at first

5. **行人**（ㄒㄧㄥˊ ㄖㄣˊ；shíngrén）

   N：a pedestrian；a person proceeding on foot
   紅燈亮的時候，行人應該等。
   When the red light is on, pedestrians should wait.

6. **舒舒服服**（ㄕㄨ ㄕㄨ ㄈㄨˊ ㄈㄨˊ；shūshūfúfú）

   SV (AABB)：very comfortable
   他過著舒舒服服的日子。
   His days pass very comfortably.
   He lives a very comfortable life.

第七課　擡驢進城

7. 辛辛苦苦地（ㄒㄧㄣ ㄒㄧㄣ ㄎㄨˇ ㄎㄨˇ ˙ㄉㄜ；shīnshīnkǔkǔde）

　　SV (AABB)：laboriously; with great efforts.
　　他辛辛苦苦地工作了二十年。
　　He has worked hard and bitterly for twenty years.

8. 疼愛（ㄊㄥˊ ㄞˋ；téng-ài）

　　FV：to be fond of (a child)
　　她太疼愛她的孩子了。
　　She is very fond of her children.

9. 趕緊（ㄍㄢˇ ㄐㄧㄣˇ；gǎnjǐn）

　　A：quickly; with no loss of time.
　　你趕緊走吧。
　　You had better hurry up and go.

10. 不像話（ㄅㄨˊ ㄒㄧㄤˋ ㄏㄨㄚˋ；búshiànghuà）

　　SV：too ridiculous !
　　outside normal and acceptable social behavior
　　你最近的行為實在太不像話了。
　　Recently your behavior has just been too much.

11. 老爹（ㄌㄠˇ ㄉㄧㄝ；lǎudiē）

　　N：father; respectful address for an aged man.

12. 吆喝（ㄧㄠ ˙ㄏㄜ；yāuhe）

　　FV：to shout; to hawk.

13. 啊哈（ㄚ ㄏㄚ；āhā）

   ON：an expression the same in pronunciation and meaning as the English "Ah ha!"

14. 竟（ㄐㄧㄥˋ；jìng）

   A：rather unexpectedly；in a way thought to be rather unlikely
   世上竟有這樣的壞人！
   How can the world have this kind of bad person?

15. 牲口（ㄕㄥ ㄎㄡˇ；shēngkǒu）

   N：livestock

16. 勁兒（ㄐㄧㄣˋㄦ；jìeer）

   N：vigor；energy；enthusiasm
   他做事很有勁兒。
   He does things with a lot of vigor.

17. 惹（ㄖㄜˇ；rě）

   FV：to provoke；to rouse；to cause
   別惹麻煩了！
   Don't cause trouble.
   是他惹老師生氣的。
   It was he that made the teacher angry.

18. 乾脆（ㄍㄢ ㄘㄨㄟˋ；gāntsuèi）

   SV：might as well；forward straight
   今晚乾脆不要做飯了，出去吃吧。

Tonight we might as well as not cook, but go out to eat.
這個人做事非常乾脆。
This person does things very straight forwardly.
A：simply and without hesitation or mincing words

19. 曲（ㄑㄩ；chiū）

FV：to bend；bend；winding；crooked

20. 吃力（ㄔ ㄌㄧˋ；chr̄li）

SV：tired；exhausted；tiring and tough (work)
這件工作對我來說很吃力。
This job is really tough for me.
FV：take a lot of doing

21. 虐待（ㄋㄩㄝˋ ㄉㄞˋ；niuèdài）

FV：to maltreat；to torment
我們不應該虐待動物。
We shouldn't maltreat animals.

22. 倒（ㄉㄠˋ；dàu）

FV：to invert；to turn upside down；to put in reverse.
把這個東西倒過來放。
Put this thing the other way up.

23. 綁（ㄅㄤˇ；bǎng）

FV：to tie；to bind

24. 根（ㄍㄣ；gēn）

M：measure word for things of slender shape, such as a

stick, spear, a piece of string, rope, etc.)

25. 粗 (ㄘㄨ ; tsū)
    SV：thick ; coarse ; rough ; crude

26. 扛 (ㄎㄤˊ ; káng)
    FV：to carry something heavy on the shoulder(s)

27. 肩膀 (ㄐㄧㄢ ㄅㄤˇ ; jiānbǎng)
    N：the shoulder(s)
    我的肩膀好酸。
    My shoulders are sore.

28. 似乎 (ㄙˋ ㄏㄨ ; sźhū)
    A：it seems, or appears that
    他似乎很生氣的樣子。
    He appears to be very angry.

29. 細加品嚼 (ㄒㄧˋ ㄐㄧㄚ ㄆㄧㄣˇ ㄐㄩㄝˊ ; shìjiāpǐnjiué)
    IE：careful and meticulous appraisal and tasting
    中國菜要細加品嚼，才能吃出味道來。
    Only when Chinese food is carefully tasted will the flavour come out.

30. 妥當 (ㄊㄨㄛˇ ㄅㄤˋ ; tuǒdàng)
    SV：appropriate ; secure ; ready
    我的說辭妥當不妥當？
    Is my statement appropriate?

第七課　擅驢進城

31. 措施（ㄘㄨㄛˋ ㄕ；tsuòshr）

   N：a measure (political, financial, etc.)
   政府的措施都是為人民著想。
   Government measures are for the sake of the people.

32. 處理（ㄔㄨˇ ㄌㄧˇ；chǔlǐ）

   FV：to deal with；to handle
   這件事讓我來處理好了。
   Let me handle this matter.

33. 失當（ㄕ ㄉㄤˋ；shrdàng）

   SV：improper；A：improperly
   那是一個失當的措施。
   That is an improper measure.

34. 擱置（ㄍㄜ ㄓˋ；gējr）

   FV：to shelve or pigeonhole (a plan, proposal, etc)

II. 成　語

1. 手足無措（ㄕㄡˇ ㄗㄨˊ ㄨˊ ㄘㄨㄛˋ；shǒutzúwútsuò）

   to be at a loss for what to do；all in a fluster
   我常常手足無措。
   I'm often at a loss for what to do.

2. 荒謬無稽（ㄏㄨㄤ ㄇㄧㄡˋ ㄨˊ ㄐㄧ；huāngmiòuwújī）

   (Lit) preposterous；absurd and unfounded (sheer nonsense)
   那是一部荒謬無稽的電影。

That is an absurd movie.

3. 耳朵軟（ㄦˇ ㄉㄨㄛ ㄖㄨㄢˇ；ěrduoruǎn）

gullible；credulous；easily convinced；tending to believe too readily

你老是耳朵軟，那麼容易相信別人。

You're always gullible, so ready to believe other people.

4. 人說東就向東，人說西就向西（ㄖㄣˊ ㄕㄨㄛ ㄉㄨㄥ ㄐㄧㄡˋ ㄒㄧㄤˋ ㄉㄨㄥ，ㄖㄣˊ ㄕㄨㄛ ㄒㄧ ㄐㄧㄡˋ ㄒㄧㄤˋ ㄒㄧ；rénshuōdūngjioùshiàngdūng, rénshuōshījioù shiàngshī）

to do everything people tell you to do

不要人說東就向東，人說西就向西，那太盲目了。

Don't do everything people tell you to do. That's too blind.

III. 練 習

1. 用下列詞語造句：

   1) 驢子
   2) 父親
   3) 兒子
   4) 辦法
   5) 兩個人
   6) 動物
   7) 肩膀
   8) 故事

9)世界
10)意見

2. 回答下列問題：

1)這一對父子帶著什麼動物進城？
2)起先，誰騎在驢背上？誰在路上走？
3)路人怎麼批評做父親的呢？
4)後來，他們怎麼辦呢？
5)路人又怎麼批評做兒子的呢？
6)後來，他們又怎麼辦呢？
7)路上的行人又怎麼笑他們呢？
8)他們一起騎在驢背上，路人又怎麼罵他們呢？
9)最後，他們怎麼做才把驢子擡進城裡了？
10)這篇故事告訴我們一個怎麼樣的道理？

第八課　井底之蛙

　　有一隻沒有見過世面的青蛙，住在小水井裡。因爲牠時常可以到水井邊、欄杆上，跳來跳去，看看外面的世界，就自以爲了不起，知識廣博，懂得比別人多。牠回到井裡，把外面的花花世界得意洋洋地告訴小蝌蚪。牠說：「有許多女人在井邊打水，洗衣服，聊天兒，還有些小孩子在唱歌，玩遊戲。」小蝌蚪聽得入迷，羨慕極了，也想出去看看。

　　有一天，到過渤海的大烏龜，到了這小水井邊，和青蛙見了面。青蛙請牠把這次旅行的見聞告訴牠。大烏龜說：「洪水隨著秋雨來了，無數溪流的水灌進了黃河，河面加寬了許多，左右兩岸有許多鄉村的綠疇，熱鬧的城市，有成千上萬的牛馬，有來來往往的車輛。

82 中國寓言故事

你生活在這個小地方,又哪兒知道外面還有許多鄉村、城市?生活在這個國家,又哪兒知道外面還有許多和我們不同的國家?我們生活在這個亞洲,越過海洋,還有美洲。我們生活在這個地球,越過太空,還有其他星球。生存在這個宇宙,還有其他宇宙。人處在地球上,不過是一個小麥粒罷了;臺灣在宇宙間,又何嘗不是一顆小麥粒呢?人跟宇宙萬物相比,也不過是牛身上的一根小毫毛罷了!」

　　大海龜這番大道理,把青蛙說得一愣一愣的,驚訝無比,所以在中國,譏笑見識淺薄、眼光如豆的人,就說他是「井底之蛙」。

　　一個人眼光的大小,學識的高低,和他的見聞有密切的關係。要增廣一個人的知識見聞,最好到世界各地去旅行觀光。

Ⅰ. 生字與生詞

1. 欄杆（ㄌㄢˊ ㄍㄢ；lángān）
   N：a railing

2. 了不起（ㄌㄧㄠˇ ㄅㄨˋ ㄑㄧˇ；liǎubùchǐ）
   SV：excellent；very good；incredible；amazing；extraordinary；terrific
   他自以爲了不起。
   He thinks he's really excellent.

3. 知識（ㄓ ㄕˋ；jrshr）
   N：knowledge
   知識就是力量。
   Knowledge is power.

4. 廣博（ㄍㄨㄤˇ ㄅㄛˊ；guǎngbó）
   SV：wide；extensive (knowledge)
   他的知識很廣博。
   His knowledge is very extensive.

5. 蝌蚪（ㄎㄜ ㄉㄡˇ；Kēdǒu）
   N：a tadpole

6. 玩遊戲（ㄨㄢˊ ㄧㄡˊ ㄒㄧˋ；wányóushì）
   VO：to play games
   小孩子最喜歡玩遊戲了。
   Children like to play games most.

7. 羨慕（ㄒㄧㄢˋ ㄇㄨˋ；shiànmù）

　　FV：to envy；to admire
　　你羨慕那些能自由自在生活的人嗎？
　　Do you envy those people who can live a carefree life？

8. 渤海（ㄅㄛˊ ㄏㄞˇ；bóhǎi）

　　N：Bóhǎi；the gulf between Liáu-dūng（遼東）and Shān-dūng（山東）peninsulas

9. 烏龜（ㄨ ㄍㄨㄟ；wūguēi）

　　N：龜　a turtle

10. 洪水（ㄏㄨㄥˊ ㄕㄨㄟˇ；húngshuěi）

　　N：flood；a deluge
　　颱風很容易帶來洪水。
　　Typhoons can easily bring deluges.

11. 加寬（ㄐㄧㄚ ㄎㄨㄢ；jiākuān）

　　FV：to broaden；to be widened
　　這條路需要加寬。
　　This road needs to be widened.

12. 岸（ㄢˋ；àn）

　　N：the bank (of a river)；the coast (of the sea)
　　臺灣東部的海岸很美。
　　The East Coast of Taiwan is very beautiful.

13. 熱鬧（ㄖㄜˋ ㄋㄠˋ；rè-nàu）

SV：noisy and bustling (place)
現在城裡最熱鬧的地方在那裡？
Where is the most bustling place in town now？

14. 車輛（ㄔㄜ ㄌㄧㄤˋ；chēliàng）

N：vehicles
台北市的車輛實在太多了。
Taipei city really has too many vehicles.
輛　M：measure word for cars

15. 亞洲（ㄧㄚˋ ㄓㄡ；yàjōu）

N：Asia；the Asian continent
中國和日本都是亞洲的國家。
China and Japan are both Asian countries.
洲　N：a continent

16. 海洋（ㄏㄞˇ ㄧㄤˊ；hǎiyáng）

N：the ocean
夜裡海洋很神秘。
The ocean at night is very mysterious.

17. 地球（ㄉㄧˋ ㄑㄧㄡˊ；dìchióu）

N：the planet earth
地球距離月亮有多遠？
How far is the earth from the moon？
球　B：a ball；a sphere

18. 太空（ㄊㄞˋ ㄎㄨㄥ；tàikūng）

N：space

太空人是美國人的英雄。
Astronauts are American's heroes.

19. 星球（ㄒㄧㄥ ㄑㄧㄡˊ；shīngchióu）

N：planets；stars
太陽系有九大星球。
The solar system has nine large planets.

20. 宇宙（ㄩˇ ㄓㄡˋ；yǔjòu）

N：the universe
我們的世界只是宇宙的一小部分。
Our world is but a small part of the universe.

21. 處在（ㄔㄨˇ ㄗㄞˋ；chǔtzài）

FV：living in；situated in
我們處在一個被污染的世界。
We live in a polluted world.

22. 小麥粒（ㄒㄧㄠˇ ㄇㄞˋ ㄌㄧˋ；shiǎumàilì）

N：a grain of wheat
小麥　wheat

23. 何嘗（ㄏㄜˊ ㄔㄤˊ；hécháng）

A：How (could it be an exception)
他笑別人笨，他又何嘗不是呢？
He laughs at others for being stupid. How could it be that he isn't?

24. 萬物（ㄨㄢˋ ㄨˋ；wànwù）

N：all things under the sun；all of creation
春天到時，萬物就從冬眠中醒來。
When spring has come, all creation wakes from winter sleep.

25. 相比（ㄒㄧㄤ ㄅㄧˇ；shiāngbǐ）

FV：to compare with each other；to make a comparison
我的聰明不能和你相比。
My intelligence can not be compared with yours.

26. 毫毛（ㄏㄠˊ ㄇㄠˊ；háumáu）

N：fine hair

27. 驚訝（ㄐㄧㄥ ㄧㄚˋ；jīngyà）

SV：to be amazed；to be astonished； be surprised；be alarmed（一般譯作驚異）
我聽到這個消息就很驚訝。
I was astonished to hear this news.

28. 無比（ㄨˊ ㄅㄧˇ；wúbǐ）

SV： 1)incomparable；without comparison；extremely matchless
2)tremendous；tremendous determination
他父親的過世，令他哀痛無比。
His father's passing away caused him to feel extremely anguished.

29. 譏笑（ㄐㄧ ㄒㄧㄠˋ；jīshiàu）

FV：to ridicule；to laugh at；to make fun at

不要譏笑我，好不好？
Don't laugh at me, O.K.?

30. 眼光（ㄧㄢˇ ㄍㄨㄤ; yǎnguāng）

   N：discerning ability；power of judgement；taste；state of attention
   他很有眼光。
   He has good taste.

31. 見聞（ㄐㄧㄢˋ ㄨㄣˊ; jiànwén）

   N：one's experience (of life)；what one has seen and heard；general knowledge
   請把你的旅途見聞，說給大家聽。
   Please tell everyone of your travel experiences.

32. 密切（ㄇㄧˋ ㄑㄧㄝˋ; michiè）

   AT：close or intimate (of relations, contact, etc.)
   中國文化和儒家思想有密切的關係。
   Chinese culture and Confucianism are intimately related.

33. 增廣（ㄗㄥ ㄍㄨㄤˇ; tzēngguǎng）

   FV：to broaded (extend)
   to widen (one's knowledge etc)；to enlarge
   要增廣見識最好的方法就是旅行。
   The best way to expand one's knowledge is by travelings.

II. 成　語

1. 井底之蛙（ㄐㄧㄥˇ ㄉㄧˇ ㄓ ㄨㄚ; jǐngdǐjrwā）

90　中國寓言故事

the frog at the bottom of the well (a frog in a well);
a person of (with a) limited outlook and experience
他什麼都不知道，像一個井底之蛙。
He doesn't know anything, just like the frog at the bottom of the well.

2. 花花世界（ㄏㄨㄚ ㄏㄨㄚ ㄕˋ ㄐㄧㄝˋ；huāhuāshìjiè）

the gay and material world; the mortal world; the dazzling human world with its myriad temptations
外面的花花世界吸引著很多人。
The gay and material world outside attracts many people.

3. 得意洋洋（ㄉㄜˊ ㄧˋ ㄧㄤˊ ㄧㄤˊ；déyìyángyáng）

complacent(ly); feeling so satisfied with oneself; the air of one who feels (sometimes unwarranted) great satisfaction, pride and pleasure at his own personality, accomplishments, or situation
他最近看起來一副得意洋洋的樣子。
Recently, he was appeared to be very self-satisfied.

4. 成千上萬（ㄔㄥˊ ㄑㄧㄢ ㄕㄤˋ ㄨㄢˋ；chéngchiānshàngwàn）

countless; numerous; hundreds upon thousands; tens of thousands
每天有成千上萬的人想賺錢。
Every day there are a countless number of people who want to make money.

5. 來來往往（ㄌㄞˊ ㄌㄞˊ ㄨㄤˇ ㄨㄤˇ；láilaiwǎngwǎng）

FV：coming and going (in great numbers)
我每天看見台北來來往往的車輛就覺得頭痛。
It gives me a headache to see the coming and going of vehicles in Taipei every day.

6. 一楞一楞（ㄧˊ ㄌㄥˋ ㄧˊ ㄌㄥˋ；yílèngyílèng）

SV：to be taken aback；be dumbfounded
他聽得一楞一楞的。
He was taken aback on hearing it.

7. 見識淺薄（ㄐㄧㄢˋ ㄕˋ ㄑㄧㄢˇ ㄅㄛˊ；jiànshŕchiǎnbó）

IE：superficial knowledge and experience
那些見識淺薄的人，每天只想賺錢，什麼也不在乎。
Those shallow people only think about making money every day, not caring about anything else.

8. 眼光如豆（ㄧㄢˇ ㄍㄨㄤ ㄖㄨˊ ㄉㄡˋ；yǎnguāngrúdòu）

IE：(Lit.) The eyesight is as big as a bean
(see no further than one's nose.)
short–sighted；to lack insight or vision.
眼光如豆的人只顧眼前，不顧未來。
People who are lacking vision are only concerned with what's ahead of them, and do not care about the future.

III. 練 習

1. 用下列詞語造句：

   1)知識

2)廣博

3)外面

4)渤海

5)旅行

6)溪流

7)鄉村

8)熱鬧

9)海洋

10)成千上萬

2. 回答下列問題：

1)一個人的學識與他的見聞有沒有關係？
2)故事裡的青蛙住在那裡？
3)牠是怎麼樣的一隻青蛙？
4)外面世界，在青蛙眼裡是怎麼樣的一個世界？
5)故事裡的大烏龜到過那裡？
6)外面世界，在大烏龜的眼裡又是一個怎麼樣的世界？
7)大烏龜看到渤海，又是一種怎麼樣的情況？
8)大烏龜最後說了一番大道理。你能夠把它重說一遍嗎？
9)大烏龜說：「人只是一顆小麥粒，只是一根小毫毛。」你同意不同意牠這種說法？
10)你讀完了「井底之蛙」這篇故事，是不是也想到各地去旅行？藉著旅行來增廣你的見識呢？

第九課　害人反害己

　　從前有一位王子，在他的父親死後，繼承了王位。他的朋友中，有兩個人的才能非常傑出；一個是建築師，一個是藝術家。他們都認為國王特別寵愛對方，而互相嫉妒。藝術家就一心想除去那個建築師。

　　有一天，藝術家偽造了一封信，對國王說：「這封信是從天上來的，是先王寄給陛下的。先王說他在天上的生活很幸福。現在想建造一座宮殿，需要一位傑出的建築師來設計，希望你立刻派遣你的建築師來。派人上天的方法很簡單，就是堆起木柴，讓建築師站在柴堆中，然後點起火來，他就會隨著煙上天。宮殿一完工，我就立刻送他回來。」

　　國王馬上召見建築師，把這事告訴他。建

94 中國寓言故事

築師聽了，就猜到這是誰的毒計，答應說：「好吧，我樂意去，替先王設計宮殿。不過，請陛下准許我回去料理後事。一個星期後，我就上天去。」國王答應了他的請求。

建築師回家後，立刻挖掘地道，從自己的臥室，直挖到打麥場。地道的出口的薄石板是可以掀開的。過了一個禮拜，建築師就在打麥場的中央，堆了濕麥桿；他站在麥桿上，叫人在自己的四周，堆起木柴，遮住他的身子，然後再叫人點火，木柴就燒了起來；建築師趕快把濕麥桿扒開，掀起石板，鑽進地道，再蓋上石板，從地道逃回家中。木柴最後完全燒成了灰燼。

建築師躲在家中的密室裡，整整一個月才出來。因爲長期沒有接觸到陽光，皮膚變得非常白皙。

建築師穿著白色的衣服，進宮去見國王，說他自己剛從天上回來，又帶回了一封先王給

國王的信，說：

「宮殿已經完工；現在需要加上一些壁畫，因為天上沒有好畫家；所以希望你再用上次的辦法，趕緊派遣身邊的藝術家來！」

國王立刻召見藝術家，要他上天去替先王畫壁畫。不消說，當人們點起木柴，他就真的被燒死了。

Ⅰ. 生字與生詞

1. 王子 (ㄨㄤˊ ㄗˇ ; wángtz)
N：a prince

2. 繼承 (ㄐㄧˋ ㄔㄥˊ ; jìchéng)
FV：to succeed to；to inherit
國王死後，王子繼承了王位。
After the king died, the prince succeeded to the throne.

3. 傑出 (ㄐㄧㄝˊ ㄔㄨ ; jiéchū)
SV：outstanding；eminent
他在學校的成績很傑出。
His accomplishments at school are outstanding.

4. 建築師 (ㄐㄧㄢˋ ㄓㄨˊ ㄕ ; jiànjúshr)
N：an architect
他是一個非常傑出的建築師。
He is an outstanding architect.

5. 藝術家 (ㄧˋ ㄕㄨˋ ㄐㄧㄚ ; yìshùjiā)
N：an artist
藝術　N：art

6. 寵愛 (ㄔㄨㄥˇ ㄞˋ ; chǔng-ài)
FV：to favor or patronize；to dote on；favorite
我是父母最寵愛的孩子。
I am my parents' favorite child.

7. 對方（ㄉㄨㄟˋ ㄈㄤ；duèi fāng）

N：the other side or party
我從對方的手上拿到一份重要的合約。
I obtained an improtant contract from the other party.

8. 一心（ㄧˋ ㄒㄧㄣ；yìshīn）

wholeheartedly
A：having one purpose；bent on (doing something)；single minded
他一心想做一個藝術家。
He is bent on being an artist.

9. 除去（ㄔㄨˊ ㄑㄩˋ；chú chiù）

FV：to get rid of
如果能把壞人都除去的話，天下就太平了。
If we could get rid of bad people, then there would be peace on earth.

10. 偽造（的）（ㄨㄟˋ ㄗㄠˋ；wèitzàu）

FV：to forge；to counterfeit；forged
AT：這是偽造的文件。
This is a forged document.

11. 先王（ㄒㄧㄢ ㄨㄤˊ；shiānwáng）

N：the late king

12. 陛下（ㄅㄧˋ ㄒㄧㄚˋ；bìshià）

N：Your Majesty

13. 座（ㄗㄨㄛˋ；tzuò）

M：measure word for mountains, bridges, buildings, etc.

14. 宮殿（ㄍㄨㄥ ㄉㄧㄢˋ；gūngdiàn）

N：a palace
這是座美麗的宮殿。
This is a beautiful palace.

15. 設計（ㄕㄜˋ ㄐㄧˋ；shèjì）

FV：to plan；to design
N：a design
她下個月將去法國學服裝設計。
She's going to France next month to study fashion design.

16. 立刻（ㄌㄧˋ ㄎㄜˋ；lìkè）

A：immediately
你爸爸打電話來要你立刻回家。
Your father phoned and wanted you to return home immediately.

17. 派遣（ㄆㄞˋ ㄑㄧㄢˇ；pàichiǎn）

FV：to dispatch；to assign；to be assigned；to be sent
他被公司派遣到日本去受訓。
He was sent by his company to Japan for job training.

18. 堆（ㄉㄨㄟ；duēi）

FV：to heap up；to pile；a heap；a pile
小孩子喜歡在海灘上堆沙。

Children enjoy piling sand on the beach.
M：heap；pile；crowd

19. 木柴（ㄇㄨˋ ㄔㄞˊ；mùchái）

N：firewood
這些木柴有點濕，沒辦法生火。
This firewood is a little wet, there's no way to start a fire.

20. 點（ㄉㄧㄢˇ；diǎn）

FV：to light；to ignite
替別人點香煙是種禮貌。
Lighting a cigarette for someone is a courtesy.

21. 煙（ㄧㄢ；yān）

N：smoke
有煙必有火。
There's no smoke without fire.

22. 召見（ㄓㄠˋ ㄐㄧㄢˋ；jàujiàn）

FV：to summon (a subordinate)； to be summoned (by a superior)；a summons
他受到總統的召見。
He received a summons from the President.

23. 猜（ㄘㄞ；tsāi）

FV：to guess
猜猜看！
Take a guess.

第九課　害人反害己　101

24. 毒計（ㄉㄨˊ ㄐㄧˋ；dújì）

   N：a malicious plan
   你要小心他的毒計。
   You need to be careful of (cautious against) his malicious plan.
   毒：N：poison；toxin；harm；malice；to poison
   BF：poisonous；malicious

25. 樂意（ㄌㄜˋ ㄧˋ；lèyì）

   SV：willing to；glad to
   我很樂意教你英文。
   I'll be glad to teach you English.

26. 准許（ㄓㄨㄣˇ ㄒㄩˇ；juěnshiǔ）

   FV：to permit；to allow
   爸爸不准許我嫁給他。
   My father doesn't permit me to marry him.

27. 臥室（ㄨㄛˋ ㄕˋ；wòshr̀）

   N：a bedroom
   這個房子只有一間臥室。
   This house has only one bedroom.

28. 打麥場（ㄉㄚˇ ㄇㄞˋ ㄔㄤˊ；dǎmàicháng）

   N：a place for threshing wheat or barley.

29. 薄（ㄅㄛˊ 或 ㄅㄠˊ；bó or báu）

   SV：thin；light

這件衣服質料很薄，很涼快。
The material of this piece of clothing is thin and cool.

30. 石板（ㄕˊ ㄅㄢˇ；shŕbǎn）

    N：a stone slab；a slate

31. 中央（ㄓㄨㄥ ㄧㄤ；jūngyāng）

    N：the center
    他站在舞台的中央。
    He is standing in the center of the stage.

32. 濕（ㄕ；shī）

    SV：wet；damp；moist；to get wet
    因爲我沒帶雨傘，所以全身都濕了。
    As I didn't take an umbrella, I was all wet.

33. 麥桿（ㄇㄞˋ ㄍㄢˇ；màigǎn）

    N：stalks of wheat or barley

34. 四周（ㄙˋ ㄓㄡ；szjōu）

    N：on all sides；all around；surroundings
    在這公園的四周種了許多樹。
    There are many trees planted on all sides of this park.

35. 遮住（ㄓㄜ ㄓㄨˋ；jējù）

    RC：to cover；to block
    當你看到烏雲遮住了太陽，大概就快下雨了。
    When you see the clouds have covered the sun, then it will probably rain soon.

36. 燒（ㄕㄠ；shāu）

FV：to burn
她把她以前的情書全都燒了。
She burned all of her past love letters.

37. 扒（ㄆㄚˊ；pá）

FV：to scratch；to claw；to dig up
那集小狗正在扒土挖洞。
That puppy is clawing up earth to dig a hole.

38. 掀起（ㄒㄧㄢ ㄑㄧˇ；shiānchǐ）

RE：to lift up； to stir；to cause；to rise
阿拉伯女人不可以掀起頭紗和男人說話。
Arabian women aren't allowed to lift up their veils and talk with men.

39. 鑽（ㄗㄨㄢ；tzuān）

FV：to penetrate；to dig through；to pierce
這個房間的牆上有一個洞，老鼠可能會鑽進來。
The wall in this room has a hole. Maybe mice will squeeze through.
鑽子 （ㄗㄨㄢˋ•ㄗ；tzuàntz）
N：a drill；an awl；etc.

40. 蓋上（ㄍㄞˋ ㄕㄤˋ；gàishàng）

RC：to cover
把杯蓋蓋上，不然灰塵會掉進去。
Put the lid on, otherwise dust will fall in.

41. 灰燼（ㄏㄨㄟ ㄐㄧㄣˋ；hueijìn）
    N：ashes；embers

42. 接觸（ㄐㄧㄝ ㄔㄨˋ；jiēchù）
    FV：to make contact with；to come in contact with
    如果你常跟<u>中國</u>人接觸，你的中文就會進步。
    If you often come in contact with Chinese people, your Chinese will improve.

43. 壁畫（ㄅㄧˋ ㄏㄨㄚˋ；bìhuà）
    N：a mural；a fresco
    牆壁（ㄑㄧㄤˊ ㄅㄧˋ；chiángbì）
    N：the wall (of a building)

44. 不消說（ㄅㄨˋ ㄒㄧㄠ ㄕㄨㄛ；bùshiāushuō）
    IE：It goes without saying
    你的中文那麼好，不消說，你一定很用功。
    Your Chinese is so good. It goes without sayiag you study very hard.

II. 成　語

1. 害人反害己（ㄏㄞˋ ㄖㄣˊ ㄈㄢˇ ㄏㄞˋ ㄐㄧˇ；hàirén fǎnhàijǐ）
   (Lit,) Harming others may turn to harm oneself. (curses come home to roost.)
   one who wants to harm others, but ends up only harming himself.

他在椅子上放了一個雞蛋，想害別人坐在雞蛋上，結果他忘了這件事，自己坐在雞蛋上，真是害人反害己。

He put the egg on the chair wanting another to sit on it. However, in the end he forgot this and sat on the egg himself. This really is harming yourself instead of harming others.

2. 互相嫉妒（ㄏㄨˋ ㄒㄧㄤ ㄐㄧˊ ㄉㄨˋ；hùshiāngjídù）

jealousy of each other；mutual jealousy

那兩個姊妹喜歡互相嫉妒。

Those two sisters like to be jealous of each other.

互相　A：mutually；reciprocally；each other

3. 料理後事（ㄌㄧㄠˋ ㄌㄧˇ ㄏㄡˋ ㄕˋ；liàulǐhòushr̀）

to take care of matters after a person's death；make arrangement for a funeral.

他雖然沒有小孩，但在他死後，他的鄰居替他料理後事。

Although he doesn't have any children, after he died, his neighbours took care of matters for him.

III. 詞組與句型

1. 因為…，所以

Because…，

因為我很忙，所以沒空打電話給你。

Because I've been busy, I've had no time to call you.

因為她沒錢，所以沒和妳去逛街購物。

She didn't go shopping with you, because she had no money.

IV. 練 習

1. 用下列詞語造句：

    1)他的
    2)他們
    3)他
    4)你
    5)你的
    6)我
    7)誰的
    8)自己的
    9)他自己
    10)人們

2. 回答下列問題：

    1)國王死後，王子繼承了什麼位置？
    2)王子有兩位朋友，各有什麼專長？
    3)這兩個朋友合得來嗎？
    4)後來，藝術家偽造了一封信來陷害建築師。你能扼要地說出這封信的內容嗎？
    5)藝術家爲什麼要偽造這封信？目的何在？
    6)建築師知道藝術家存心要燒死他；爲什麼還答應去呢？
    7)他有没有被燒死？
    8)他如何逃脫？

9)後來,他又想出什麼計謀來對付藝術家?
10)最後藝術家自食其果被燒死了;但大家會怎麼批評他?

第十課　尋求真理

　　在我們的小鎮上，有兩個富有研究精神的少年，一個叫小德，一個叫小理。他們都喜歡討論問題，凡事追根究底。下面的有趣對話，就是這樣產生的。

　　小理：小德，你說夫妻親呢？還是父母親呢？

　　小德：當然，父母跟我們親啊。

　　小理：夫妻比較親。他們生前同睡一張床上，死後同葬一個墓裡，恩恩愛愛，不是比父母更親密嗎！

　　小德：不是這樣說。父母好像樹的根本，配偶好像車的輪子。輪子壞了，可以再換新的。根本沒了，樹就要枯萎。夫妻，哪能比得上父母呢？

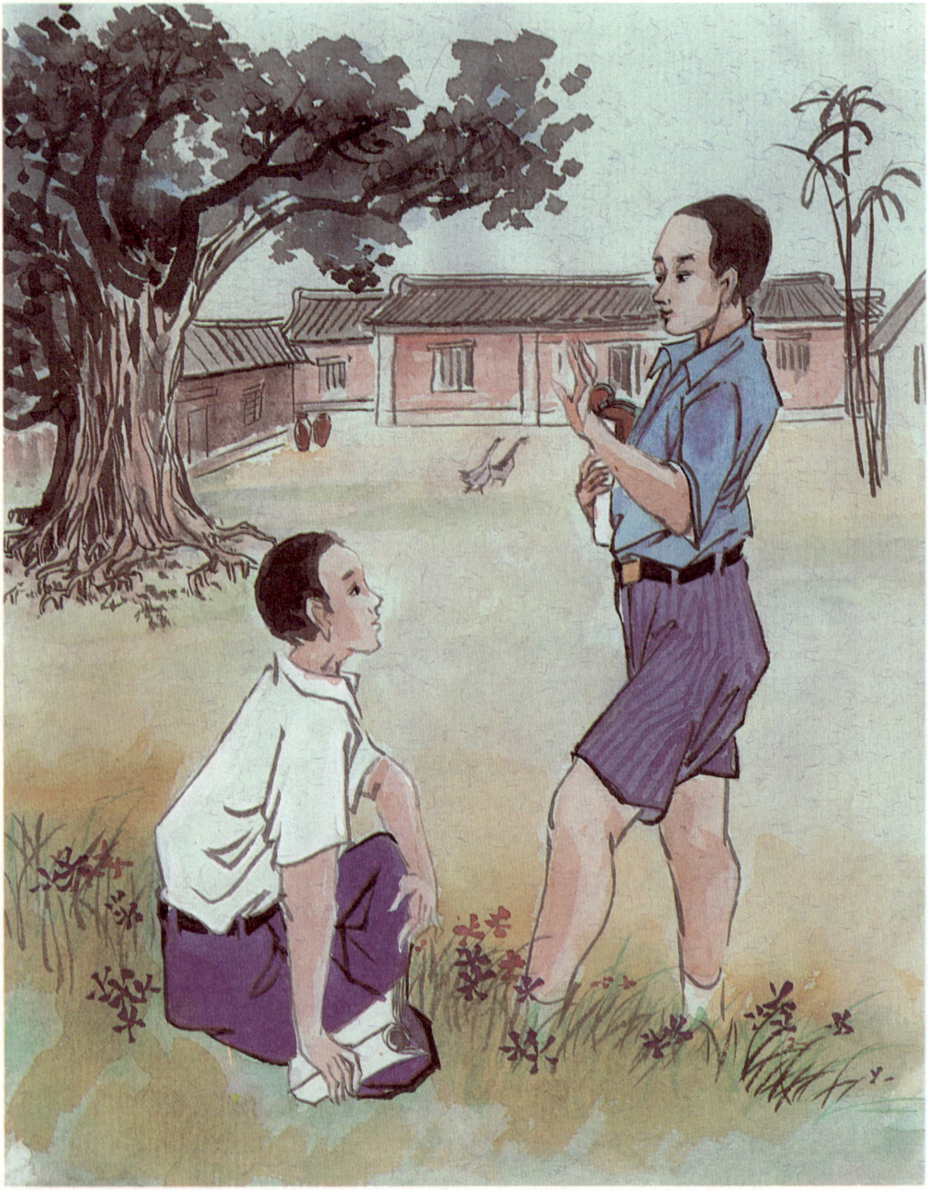

小理：鵝、鴨爲什麼會游水？螢火蟲爲什麼會發光？雁、鶴爲什麼叫聲很響亮？冬天的時候，松柏的葉子爲什麼還是綠綠的？

小德：鵝、鴨會游水，是因爲有蹼。螢火蟲會發光，是因爲尾巴帶著一盞小燈籠。雁、鶴叫聲很響亮，是因爲有長脖子。松柏的葉子，到冬天還是綠色的，是因爲有堅強的樹幹。

小理：小龜能夠在海浪中游水，那裡是因爲牠有蹼。燐火甲蟲的兩肩，各有一個發光眼，那裡是因爲牠有什麼燈籠。蝦蟆的叫聲也很響亮，那裡是脖子長。竹子常青，那裡是因爲中心堅實。

一件事，從這一點來看，有道理；從另一點來看，也有道理。所以有人說：「世間沒有絕對的真理。」他們兩人爭辯不下，就去請教鎮上最聰明的人。這位最聰明的人說：「真理只有一個。你們現在說的道理，還不是最恰

當、最正確的,你們應該繼續去追尋那唯一的真理。」

Ⅰ. 生字與生詞

1. **尋求**（ㄒㄩㄣˊ ㄑㄧㄡˊ；shiúnchioú）
   FV：to seek；to try；to get
   這個可憐的老婦人在尋求幫助。
   This poor old woman is seeking help.

2. **真理**（ㄓㄣ ㄌㄧˇ；jēnlǐ）
   N：the truth
   我們都在尋求真理。
   We are all seeking the truth.

3. **小鎮**（ㄒㄧㄠˇ ㄓㄣˋ；shiǎujèn）
   N：a town (bigger than a village, smaller than a city)

4. **研究**（ㄧㄢˊ ㄐㄧㄡˋ；yánjioù）
   FV：to make a stduy of
   他專心研究醫學。
   He is dedicated to the study of medicine.

5. **討論**（ㄊㄠˇ ㄌㄨㄣˋ；tǎuluèn）
   FV：to discuss
   我常常和同學討論功課。
   I often discuss the homework with my classmates.

6. **產生**（ㄔㄢˇ ㄕㄥ；chǎnshēng）
   FV：to be brought about；to give rise to；to produce
   你知道人口太多會產生什麼問題嗎？

Do you know what problems will be brought about by over population?

7. 夫妻（ㄈㄨ ㄑㄧ；fūchī）

N：a married couple；husband and wife
這對夫妻常常吵架。
This couple often quarrel.

8. 親（ㄑㄧㄣ；chīn）

SV：to be intimate with；to be close to
我跟我的祖母很親。
I am close to my grandmother.
他們是親近的朋友。
They are close friends.

9. 生前（ㄕㄥ ㄑㄧㄢˊ；shēngchián）

N：during one's lifetime
他生前做了許多好事，我們很懷念他。
During his lifetime he did many good things. We miss him very much.

10. 葬（ㄗㄤˋ；tzàng）

FV：to bury
他的家人把他葬在那裡？
Where did his family bury him？

11. 墓（ㄇㄨˋ；mù）

N：a grave；a tomb
他們很久沒去山上掃墓了。

They haven't been to the mountain to sweep the tomb for a long time.

12. 親密（ㄑㄧㄣ ㄇㄧˋ；chīnmì）

   SV：to be close to；to be intimate with

13. 根本（ㄍㄣ ㄅㄣˇ；gēnběn）

   N：root；base；origin；basically
   家庭是社會的根本。
   Families are the base of the society.
   A：at all；simply
   你根本不懂什麼叫做謙虛。
   Basically, you don't understand what modesty is.

14. 配偶（ㄆㄟˋ ㄡˇ；pèi-ǒu）

   N：spouse
   請你填上你配偶的名字。
   Please fill in your spouse's name.

15. 輪子（ㄌㄨㄣˊ・ㄗ；luéntz）

   N：a wheel

16. 壞（ㄏㄨㄞˋ；huài）

   SV：borken；bad；mean
   我的手錶壞了。
   My watch is broken.

17. 枯萎（ㄎㄨ ㄨㄟˇ；kūwěi）

   SV：be withered

昨天我買的玫瑰花今天就枯萎了。
The roses I bought yesterday have withered today.

18. 鵝 (ㄜˊ ; é)

N：a goose ; geese

19. 螢火蟲 (ㄧㄥˊ ㄏㄨㄛˇ ㄔㄨㄥˊ ; yínghuǒchúng)

N：a firefly.

20. 發光 (ㄈㄚ ㄍㄨㄤ ; fāguāng)

VO：to emit light ; to shine ; to glitter
螢火蟲在黑夜裡發光。
On dark nights fireflies shine.

21. 雁 (ㄧㄢˋ ; yàn)

N：wild geese

22. 鶴 (ㄏㄜˋ ; hè)

N：a crane (bird)

23. 響亮 (ㄒㄧㄤˇ ㄌㄧㄤˋ ; shiǎngliàng)

SV：loud and clear
我妹妹的聲音很響亮。
My younger sister's voice is loud and clear.

24. 松柏 (ㄙㄨㄥ ㄅㄞˇ ; sūng bǎi)

N：pine ; fir ; conifers
松：pine
柏：cypress

第十課　尋求真理　117

25. 蹼（ㄆㄨˊ；pú）

    N：webs on the feet of water fowl

26. 尾巴（ㄧˇ（ㄨㄟˇ）‧ㄅㄚ；yǐ(wěi) ba）

    N：a tail
    狗搖尾巴表示友善。
    Dogs wag their tails to express friendliness.

27. 盞（ㄓㄢˇ；jǎn）

    M：measure word for lamps

28. 燈籠（ㄉㄥ　ㄉㄨㄥˊ；dēnglúng）

    N：a lantern
    提燈籠是元宵節的一種習俗。
    Carrying lanterns is a custom on Lantern Festival.

29. 脖子（ㄅㄛˊ‧ㄗ；bótz）

    N：the neck

30. 堅強（ㄐㄧㄢ　ㄑㄧㄤˊ；jiānchiáng）

    SV：strong；firm；unyielding
    他的意志很堅強。
    He has a very strong will.

31. 燐火甲蟲（ㄌㄧㄣˊ　ㄏㄨㄛˇ　ㄐㄧㄚˇ　ㄔㄨㄥˊ；línhuǒjiǎchúng）

    N：a kind of light-emitting beetle
    甲蟲　a beetle

32. 蝦蟆（ㄏㄚˊ·ㄇㄚ；há ma）
   N：a toad

33. 常青（ㄔㄤˊ ㄑㄧㄥ；chángchīng）
   SV：evergreen
   松樹是常青的樹。
   Pines are evergreen trees.

34. 堅實（ㄐㄧㄢ ㄕˊ；jiānshŕ）
   SV：solid；strong；durable
   這棟大樓蓋得很堅實。
   This building is solidly built.

35. 這一點（ㄓㄜˋ ㄧ ㄉㄧㄢˇ；jèyidiǎn）
   PN：this point
   你對這一點有什麼看法？
   What is your opinion on this point?

36. 絕對（ㄐㄩㄝˊ ㄉㄨㄟˋ；jiuéduèi）
   AT：absolute；unconditional
   在軍隊中要求絕對服從。
   In the army, absolute obedience is required.

37. 請教（ㄑㄧㄥˇ ㄐㄧㄠˋ；chǐngjiàu）
   VO：to request instructions or advice
   我有幾個問題請教你。
   I have some questions to ask you.

第十課　尋求真理　119

38. 恰當（ㄑㄧㄚˋ ㄉㄤˋ；chiàdàng）
    SV：appropriate；fitting
    他的回答很恰當。
    His reply is very fitting.

39. 正確（ㄓㄥˋ；ㄑㄩㄝˋ；jèngchiuè）
    SV & AT：accurate；correct
    這是一個正確的答案。
    This is a correct answer.

40. 唯一（ㄨㄟˊ ㄧ；wéiyī）
    AT：the only
    我是我父母唯一的孩子。
    I am my parents' only child.

II. 成　語

1. 追根究底（ㄓㄨㄟ ㄍㄣ ㄐㄧㄡˋ ㄉㄧˇ；juēigēnjioùdǐ）
   (Lit,) get to the root and find the bottom; to get to the bottom of (something)
   他凡事喜歡追根究底。
   He likes to get to the bottom of everything.

2. 恩恩愛愛（ㄣ ㄣ ㄞˋ ㄞˋ；ēnēnàiài）
   loving and devoted (said of a couple)
   他們是一對恩恩愛愛的夫妻。
   They are a loving and devoted couple.

3. 爭辯不下（ㄓㄥ ㄅㄧㄢˋ ㄅㄨˊ ㄒㄧㄚˋ；jēngbiànbúshià）
to argue or debate without coming to a solution or result; to sticks to his own stand
他們爲了這個問題爭辯不下。
For this problem, they argued without result.

III. 詞組與句型

1. 還是⋯

still
我雖然很喜歡這裡，但我還是得離開。
Although I like here, I still have to leave.
他還是想要當歌星。
He still wants to be a singer.

2. 比得上

incomparable; to compare with
他的中文很好，比得上中國人。
His Chinese is very good. It can compare with that of a Chinese person.
沒有人比得上他的能幹。
Nobody can compare with his competence.

3. 從⋯來看

from⋯ point of view; according to (one's point of view)
請你從我的觀點來看這個問題好嗎？

Please look at this problem from my point of view, OK?

IV. 練 習

1. 用下列詞語造句：

   1)有兩個
   2)還是
   3)同
   4)比
   5)好像
   6)可以
   7)爲什麼
   8)是因爲
   9)那裡是
   10)從

2. 回答下列問題：

   1)鎮上有兩個少年；他們叫什麼名字？
   2)他們常在一起討論問題嗎？
   3)他們起先討論了什麼問題？
   4)你認爲夫妻的關係親呢？還是父母跟兒女的關係親呢？
   5)後來，他們又討論了什麼問題？
   6)鵝和鴨子爲什麼會游水？
   7)螢火蟲、燐火甲蟲爲什麼會發光？

8)爲什麼雁、鶴和蝦蟆的叫聲很響亮呢？
9)爲什麼到冬天松、柏和竹子的葉子還是常青不落呢？
10)大家對事情的看法一致嗎？那麼，我們應該如何去探求一件事情的真理？

第十一課　除禍要趁早

村裡有個年輕人，天天都在想賺錢發財。

有一天，鄰居張老爹給了他一個雞蛋。他高興得不得了，整晚都睡不著覺，連夜擬好一個計畫，還叫醒他妻子對她說：「老婆呀老婆，你聽我說，現在我有本錢了，我要發財了！」

妻子問他：「你的本錢在哪裡？你哪裡來的本錢？」

這個年輕人說：「張老爹給我的雞蛋，就是我的本錢呀！大概只要十年，我們就可以擁有一所具有相當規模的畜牧場了。」他接著又說：

「我們可以借鄰家的母雞，把這個雞蛋孵出來。等三個月，小母雞長大了，就開始生

124　中國寓言故事

蛋；每個月生二、三十個蛋，就可以孵出二、三十隻小雞。再三個月，這些小雞長大又開始生蛋，蛋又孵出雞。雞生蛋，蛋孵雞，一年後就可以有一萬隻雞了。我們把一部分雞賣掉，買五頭牛。牛又生牛；大概再三年，就可以有幾百頭牛了，成爲一個小畜牧場。我們再把一部分的雞和牛賣掉，擴充設備；這樣，不要十年，我就可以成爲一個小企業家了。並僱用許多工人幫我養雞、養牛了。我的錢多了，我還可以娶一個小老婆，幫妳料理家事；妳可以跟我過舒舒服服的生活了！」

他的妻子聽他說要娶小老婆，非常生氣，說：「還沒發財，就要娶小老婆！」一巴掌就把這一個雞蛋拍得稀爛，說：「不要留下禍根！」

丈夫眼看他的美夢被妻子打得粉碎，一怒之下，到法院控告他的妻子敗光了他的財產，要求法官判她重罪。

法官問：「哦，你說說看；她是怎樣把你的財產敗光了的？」

　　這個人就把事情經過說了一遍。法官說：「這樣一大筆的財產，壞在太太的一掌，的確可惡，應判重罪。」

　　妻子說：「可是這都還是沒有發生的事啊。爲什麼要判我罪呢？」

　　法官說：「你先生說娶小老婆，也是還沒有發生的事情，你爲什麼要嫉妒呢？」

　　妻子說：「雖然，還沒有發生，但是除禍要趁早呀！」

　　法官聽了，就釋放了她。

Ⅰ. 生字與生詞

1. 除禍（ㄔㄨˊ ㄏㄨㄛˋ；chúhuò）

    VO：to get rid of trouble and ruin
    警察的工作就是為民除暴。
    The police's job is to get rid of the violence for people.

2. 趁早（ㄔㄣˋ ㄗㄠˇ；chèntzǎu）

    A：(to act) before it is too late；as early as possible.
    你應該趁早完成學業，否則日後會後悔。
    You should complete your studies before it's too late otherwise you will regret it afterwards.
    趁　FV：to take advantage of；to avail oneself of

3. 發財（ㄈㄚ ㄘㄞˊ；fātsái）

    VO：to become rich
    有很多人天天只想發財。
    There are many people who only think about becoming rich every day.
    財　N：wealth；riches

4. 鄰居（ㄌㄧㄣˊ ㄐㄩ；línjiū）

    N：neighbor(s)
    我和我的鄰居不太熟。
    I don't know my neighbors very well.

5. 連夜（ㄌㄧㄢˊ ㄧㄝˋ；liányè）

    A：all through the night

6. 擬（ㄋㄧˇ；nǐ）

    FV：to plan；to intend；to decide；to determine
    讓我們先為這個周末擬一個計畫。
    Let's first work out a plan for the weekend.

7. 叫醒（ㄐㄧㄠˋ ㄒㄧㄥˇ；jiàushǐng）

    RC：to waken
    請你在明天早上叫醒我。
    Please wake me up tomorrow morning.

8. 老婆（ㄌㄠˇ ㄆㄛˊ；lǎupó）

    N：a wife

9. 擁有（ㄩㄥˇ ㄧㄡˇ；yǔngyǒu）

    FV：to own
    他擁有一座農場。
    He owns a farm.

10. 所（ㄙㄨㄛˇ；suǒ）

    M：measure word for schools, charity institutes, etc.

11. 具有（ㄐㄩˋ ㄧㄡˇ；jiùyǒu）

    FV：to have
    你具有畫畫的才能嗎？
    Do you have the ability to paint？

12. 相當（ㄒㄧㄤ ㄉㄤ；shiāngdāng）

    A：very；quite；considerable

我媽媽的日文相當好。
My mother's Japanese is quite good.

13. 規模（ㄍㄨㄟ ㄇㄛˊ；guēimó）

    N：scale；magnitude；scope
    這所醫院，規模很大。
    This hospital is on a big scale.

14. 畜牧場（ㄒㄩˋ ㄇㄨˋ ㄔㄤˊ；shiùmùcháng）

    N：a livestock farm
    畜牧　FV：to raise (livestock)

15. 孵（ㄈㄨ；fū）

    FV：to hatch；to emerge from eggs or spawn
    那隻母雞正在孵蛋。
    That hen is hatching an egg.

16. 一部分（ㄧˊ ㄅㄨˋ ㄈㄣˋ；yíbùfèn）

    N：a part；a portion
    你每個月存一部分的薪水嗎？
    Do you save part of your salary every month？

17. 擴充（ㄎㄨㄛˋ ㄔㄨㄥ；kuòchūng）

    FV：to expand；expansion
    他花了十年的時間擴充他的公司。
    He spent ten years expanding his company.

18. 設備（ㄕㄜˋ ㄅㄟˋ；shèbèi）

    N：facilities；equipment

這是一所設備很好的學校。
This is a well equipped school.

19. 企業（ㄑㄧˋ ㄧㄝˋ；chìyè）

   N：enterprise；business
   他們家擁有龐大的企業。
   Their family owns a huge business.

20. 娶（ㄑㄩˇ；chiǔ）

   FV：to take a wife
   他想要娶個老婆。
   He wants to take a wife.

21. 一巴掌（ㄧ ㄅㄚ ㄓㄤˇ；yībājǎng）

   N：a palm of the hand
   拍手需要兩個巴掌，一個巴掌拍不響。
   It takes two palms to clap. A palm cannot clap.

22. 拍（ㄆㄞ；pāi）

   FV：to strike (with the hand)；to slap；to pat
   不要拍我的頭。
   Don't pat my head.

23. 稀爛（ㄒㄧ ㄌㄢˋ；shīlàn）

   SV：pulpified；like paste；crumbled
   這根香蕉被我壓得稀爛。
   This banana was squashed by me.

24. 禍根（ㄏㄨㄛˋ ㄍㄣ；huògēn）

N：root of trouble
不誠實是他生意失敗的禍根。
Dishonesty is the root of trouble for his business failure.

25. 粉碎（ㄈㄣˇ ㄙㄨㄟˋ；fěnsuèi）

    FV：to smash；completely smashed
    SV：炸彈把房子炸得粉碎。
    The bomb blow the house to pieces.
    粉　N：powder；flour
    碎　SV：broken；smashed

26. 法院（ㄈㄚˇ ㄩㄢˋ；fǎyuàn）

    N：a court of law
    他在法院上班。
    He works at the court.

27. 控告（ㄎㄨㄥˋ ㄍㄠˋ；kùnggàu）

    FV：to sue；to accuse
    我要控告你破壞我的名譽。
    I want to sue you for slander.

28. 敗光（ㄅㄞˋ ㄍㄨㄤ；bàiguāng）

    RE：used up and wasted

29. 財產（ㄘㄞˊ ㄔㄢˇ；tsáichǎn）

    N：property
    他家的財產全被他敗光了。
    All his family's property was used up and wasted by him.

30. 法官（ㄈㄚˇ ㄍㄨㄢ；fǎguān）
    N：a judge (of a court)

31. 判（ㄆㄢˋ；pàn）
    FV：to judge；to convict
    法官判他無罪。
    The judge pronounced him not guilty.

32. 重罪（ㄓㄨㄥˋ ㄗㄨㄟˋ；jùngtzuèi）
    N：serious offense
    罪　N：sin；crime；offence；fault；evil；guilt

33. 一遍（ㄧˊ ㄅㄧㄢˋ；yíbiàn）
    NU. M：one time
    請再說一遍。
    Please say that once more.

34. 的確（ㄉㄧˊ ㄑㄩㄝˋ；díchiuè）
    A：certainly；surely
    她的確很漂亮。
    She is certainly very beautiful.

35. 可惡（ㄎㄜˇ ㄨˋ；kěwù）
    SV：detestable；hateful；abhorrent
    你真可惡！
    You are abhorrent！

36. 釋放（ㄕˋ ㄈㄤˋ；shìfàng）

FV：to set free； to release
他們終於決定釋放那些人。
They finally decided to release those people.

II. 成　語

1. 一怒之下（ㄧˊ ㄋㄨˋ ㄓ ㄒㄧㄚˋ；yínùjrshià）

in a moment of anger
她在一怒之下，打了她兒子一巴掌。
In a moment of anger, she slapped her son.

III. 句　型

1. 不但⋯並且⋯

not only⋯ but also⋯
我的工作不但輕鬆並且有趣。
My job is not only relaxed, but also interesting.
他不但聰明，並且能幹。
He is not only intelligent, but also capable.

2. 雖然⋯，但是⋯

certainly⋯, however
工作雖然重要，但是健康更重要。
Work is certainly important, however health is more important.

生命雖然可貴，但是自由更爲重要。

Life is certainly precious, but freedom is more important.

IV. 練　習

1. 用下列詞語造句：

　　1)賺錢
　　2)鄰居
　　3)擬好
　　4)計畫
　　5)本錢
　　6)規模
　　7)賣掉
　　8)擴充
　　9)僱用
　　10)稀爛

2. 回答下列問題：

　　1)村裡的那個年輕人，每天都在胡思亂想些什麼？
　　2)後來，張老爹給他一個什麼好東西？
　　3)他怎麼利用一個雞蛋做資金來經營畜牧場呢？
　　4)他這一套「蛋孵雞，雞生蛋」的生產理論，有用嗎？
　　5)一年後，根據他估計：他將有多少隻雞呢？
　　6)這時候，他想賣掉一部分雞，去買什麼呢？
　　7)牛又生牛，雞又生雞，他賺了許多錢；這時，他又打算做什

麼好事？
8)他妻子聽說他有錢就要娶小老婆，就採取了什麼行動？
9)他的美夢被妻子粉碎了，他採取了什麼行動？
10)法官有沒有判他妻子的罪呢？爲什麼沒有？

第十二課　致富[1]之術

　　富先生非常富有,窮先生非常貧窮[2]。窮先生就去拜訪富先生,請教賺錢致富的方法。

　　富先生說:「我很會『偷[3]』,偷了一年,生活就過得去;兩年,就夠用;三年,就十分富有了。繼續拼命地做[4],就越來越有錢了。」

　　窮先生聽了,以為致富的秘訣[5],就是去偷人家的東西,不等富先生把話說清楚,就告辭回去了[6]。其實,他並不了解富先生偷天致富[7]的道理;所以回去之後,就真的幹起小偷來,闖空門[8],偷東西[9]。但沒有多久,就因人贓俱獲被逮捕判刑[10],不但被追回贓物[11],還要另處罰金[12]坐牢。

　　窮先生以為富先生欺騙他,出獄後[13],又去找富先生理論[14]。

- 137 -

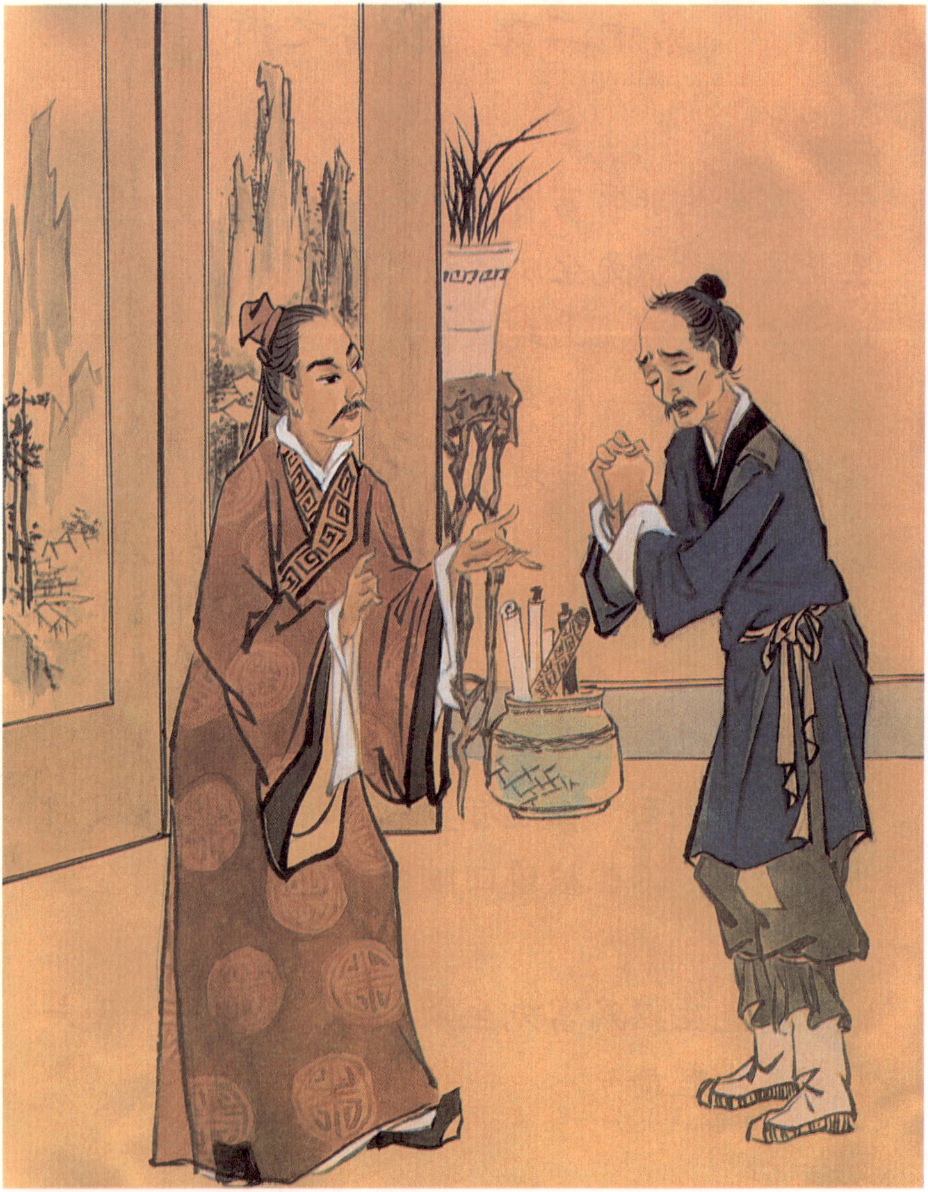

富先生說:「你怎麼去偷人家的東西呢?唉,你誤解了我說的偷的道理,我們都知道:天候有適合耕種的季節,土地蘊藏著許多資源;我所說的『偷』,就是偷適當的天時,豐富的地利,像利用春雨、陽光和土地,來種植物,養雞鴨魚蝦,還燒黏土做磚瓦,砍樹木蓋房屋。這些都是自然的產物,只要我們努力苦幹,財富就會越來越多。也可以說,我的財富都是從大自然偷來的。金錢珠寶都是別人所有,怎麼能去偷呢?觸犯刑法,被判了罪,又能怨誰?」

人要生活,怎麼能不偷?利用自然資源,製造財富,是謀生的正道;偷竊別人財物,佔為己有,是自私違法的行為。

Ⅰ. 生字與生詞

1. 致富（ㄓˋ ㄈㄨˋ；jrfù）

VO：to become rich；to acquire wealth
年輕人不應只想致富。
Young people shouldn't only think about the way of acquiring wealth.

2. 貧窮（ㄆㄧㄣˊ ㄑㄩㄥˊ；pínchiúng）

SV：poor
貧窮的人每天想著致富的方法。
Poor people think about ways to become rich every day.

3. 偷（ㄊㄡ；tōu）

FV：to steal
偷東西是犯法的行為。
Stealing (things) is illegal behaviour.

4. 拚命（ㄆㄧㄣ ㄇㄧㄥˋ；pīnmìng）

FV：going all out to do something, usually somewhat recklessly；for the sake of one's life；risk one's life
A：他拚命賺錢。
He is frantically making money.

5. 秘訣（ㄇㄧˋ ㄐㄩㄝˊ；mìjiué）

N：a knack；secrets (of success, etc)；the key (to the solution of a problem)
賺錢沒有什麼秘訣；努力工作，就能賺到錢。

There is no secret to making money; work hard and you can make money.

6. 其實（ㄑㄧˊ ㄕˊ；chíshŕ）

   MA：actually；in fact
   其實，他是個好人。
   Actually, he is a good person.

7. 了解（ㄌㄧㄠˇ ㄐㄧㄝˇ；liǎujiě）

   FV：to understand；understanding

8. 小偷（ㄒㄧㄠˇ ㄊㄡ；shiǎutōu）

   N：a thief

9. 闖空門（ㄔㄨㄤˇ ㄎㄨㄥ ㄇㄣˊ；chuǎngkūngmén）

   IE：to intrude into an unguarded house for the purpose of stealing
   闖　FV：to rush into；to intrude into

10. 判刑（ㄆㄢˋ ㄒㄧㄥˊ；pànshíng）

    FV：to sentence
    那個小偷被判刑了嗎？
    Has that thief been sentenced？

11. 贓物（ㄗㄤ ㄨˋ；tzāngwù）

    N：stolen goods
    我們不可以收賣贓物。
    We are not allowed to receive and sell stolen goods.

12. 罰金（ㄈㄚˊ ㄐㄧㄣ；fájīn）

N：a fine；to impose a fine
開快車要處多少罰金？
How much is the fine for speeding？

13. 出獄（ㄔㄨ ㄩˋ；chūyù）

FV：to get out of prison
你覺得我們應該給出獄的人工作機會嗎？
Do you think we should give people getting out of prison the opportunity to work？

14. 理論（ㄌㄧˇ ㄌㄨㄣˋ；lǐluèn）

FV：to argue；to reason
他賣給你的水果壞了，明天我去找他理論。
The fruit he sold you is bad. I'll talk to him tomorrow.
N：a theory

15. 誤解（ㄨˋ ㄐㄧㄝˇ；wùjiě）

FV：to misunderstand
你誤解我的意思了。
You misunderstand what I mean.

16. 天候（ㄊㄧㄢ ㄏㄡˋ；tiānhòu）

N：the weather

17. 耕種（ㄍㄥ ㄓㄨㄥˋ；gēngjùng）

FV：to plough and sow
農夫的工作就是耕田種地。

A farmer's job is to plough and sow the fields.

18. 季節（ㄐㄧˋ ㄐㄧㄝˊ；jìjié）

   N：a season
   春天是適合耕種的季節。
   Spring is an appropriate season for ploughing and sowing.

19. 蘊藏（ㄩㄣˋ ㄘㄤˊ；yùntsáng）

   FV：to have deposited；to have in store

20. 資源（ㄗ ㄩㄢˊ；tzyuán）

   N：natural resources；resources
   這座山裡蘊藏著金礦資源。
   This mountain contains gold deposits.

21. 天時（ㄊㄧㄢ ㄕˊ；tiānshŕ）

   N：the climate；the weather；the time

22. 地利（ㄉㄧˋ ㄌㄧˋ；dìlì）

   N：land productivity
   現在正是天時、地利、人和都好的時候，我們應該把握這個機會。
   Everything is just right. We should take this opportunity in hand. (i.e. the right time, place and people for something to be realized have all come together and complement each other)

23. 蝦（ㄒㄧㄚ；shiā）

   N：a shrimp

24. 黏土（ㄋㄧㄢˊ ㄊㄨˇ；niántǔ）

N：clay
黏　FV：to stick；sticky；adhesive；viscous

25. 磚瓦（ㄓㄨㄢ ㄨㄚˇ；juānwǎ）

N：bricks and tiles
他把黏土燒成磚瓦。
He fired(baked) the clay to make bricks and tiles in a kiln.

26. 所有（ㄙㄨㄛˇ ㄧㄡˇ；suǒyǒu）

N：possessions；belongings；own
AT：all
FV：to own；to possess
這些錢都是別人所有。
All these money belong to someone else.
我自己一無所有。
I have nothing of my own.

27. 謀生（ㄇㄡˊ ㄕㄥ；móushēng）

VO：to make a living
你靠什麼謀生？
How do you make a living？

28. 正道（ㄓㄥˋ ㄉㄠˋ；jèngdàu）

N：the proper way；the right course
努力工作才是賺錢的正道。
Working hard is the only proper way to make money.

29. 偷竊（ㄊㄡ ㄑㄧㄝˋ；tōuchiè）
    FV：to steal；stealing

30. 自私（ㄗˋ ㄙ；tzsz̄）
    SV：selfish
    他很自私。
    He is very selfish.

31. 違法（ㄨㄟˊ ㄈㄚˇ；wéifǔ）
    VO：illegal；unlawful
    偷竊是違法的。
    Stealing is illegal.

II. 成　語

1. 偷天致富（ㄊㄡ ㄊㄧㄢ ㄓˋ ㄈㄨˋ；tōutiānjr̄fù）
   to use natural resources to make a fortune
   你知道什麼叫做「偷天致富」嗎？
   Do you know what, "stealing heaven to make a fortune" means？

2. 人贓俱獲（ㄖㄣˊ ㄗㄤ ㄐㄩˋ ㄏㄨㄛˋ；réntzāngjiùhuò）
   a thief caught together with the loot
   因為人贓俱獲，所以那個小偷被逮捕了。
   Because he was caught with the loot, the thief was arrested.
   獲　to get；to obtain

3. 觸犯刑法（ㄔㄨˋ ㄈㄢˋ ㄒㄧㄥˊ ㄈㄚˇ；chùfànshíngfǎ）
   to violate criminal law
   一個良好的國民不會觸犯刑法。
   A good citizen will not violate the law.

4. 佔爲己有（ㄓㄢˋ ㄨㄟˊ ㄐㄧˇ ㄧㄡˇ；jànwéijǐyǒu）
   take forcible possession of…?
   我們不應該把別人的東西佔爲己有。
   We shouldn't take others' possession as our own.
   佔　to occupy；to usurp；to seize

III. 句組與句型

1. 不但…，還要

not only…, also need (want)
他不但要唸醫學院，還要去美國唸書。
He not only wants to study at medical school, but also to go to the USA to study.
我不但努力工作，還要節省金錢。
I not only need to work hard, but also need to be economical with my money.

IV. 練　習

1. 用下列詞語造句：

   1) 非常
   2) 請教

3)很會

4)就

5)了解

6)幹起

7)利用

8)種

9)養

10)製造

2. 回答下列問題：

1)窮先生為什麼去拜訪富先生？
2)富先生有沒有把致富的方法告訴窮先生？
3)用什麼方法可以致富？
4)窮先生真的了解富先生的「致富秘訣」嗎？
5)結果怎麼樣？
6)窮先生出獄後，為什麼又去拜訪富先生？
7)富先生又跟窮先生說些什麼？
8)富先生所說「偷天致富」，到底是怎麼樣的一種偷法？
9)可以偷的是什麼？不可以偷的是什麼？
10)那麼要想致富，應該怎麼樣去做才行？

第十三課　忘恩負義

　　東郭先生推著車子在路上走的時候，遇到一隻受傷的狼。狼說：「請您救救我，讓我躲在您車上的麻布袋裡。」東郭先生看牠怪可憐的，就答應了。獵人追過來，問他說：「你有沒有看見一隻受傷的狼？」東郭先生說：「沒看見。」

　　獵人走了。東郭先生解開袋子，把狼放出來。沒想到狼竟翻臉對他說：「我肚子餓了，我要吃你。」東郭先生說：「我救了你；你反而要吃我。哪有這種道理？」狼說：「救人要救到底；你還是讓我吃了吧！要沒有吃的，我也會餓死。」東郭先生說：「別急，別急，咱們找個人評評理。」

　　他們先去問老杏樹。東郭先生說：「老

150　中國寓言故事

杏，老杏，我救了牠，牠反要吃我；你說牠有理沒理？」老杏樹說：「這有甚麼稀奇？從前我結了許多又甜又大的杏兒，人人吃了都叫好！現在我老了，結不出杏兒來了，那些人就要砍我的樹枝兒當柴燒。」狼聽了，張嘴就要吃他。東郭先生說：「慢著，慢著，還要再問問別人看。」

他們又去問老牛。東郭先生說：「老牛，老牛，我救了牠，牠反要吃我；你說牠有理沒理？」老牛說：「狼要吃你，自然合理！我幫主人，拉車耕田；現在我老了，把我扔在這裡不管，聽說還要殺我去賣錢呢。」狼聽了，說：「這回可以吃了吧！」東郭先生說：「慢著，慢著，還要再找一個人作最後的評判。」

最後，他們問到一個老頭子。東郭先生很有禮貌地問他：「老先生，老先生，我救了狼，狼卻要吃我；你說合理不合理？」老頭兒想了想說：「也許有理。不過，先讓我調查一

下。請你們從頭表演起,讓我看看。」狼說:「他讓我躲進袋子裡,不是要救我,只是想憋死我。他没安好心,自然該死。」老頭兒說:「你說的,我没看見;怎麼能裁定誰是誰非?」狼聽了,就自己鑽進袋子裡去,說:「就是這樣子。」老頭兒說:「袋子口是開著呢,還是紮著呢?」狼說:「他把口兒紮得緊緊的,所以憋氣呀。」老頭兒說:「東郭先生,請你把袋子口兒紮緊;讓我看看,會不會憋氣?」東郭先生就把袋子口兒紮好了。

「刀呢?」老頭兒又對東郭先生說:「你還不趕快動手?」東郭先生說:「我救了牠,怎好再殺牠?」老頭兒說:「無情無義的畜生,你還跟牠講什麼人情道理呢?」

Ⅰ. 生字與生詞

1. 受傷（ㄕㄡˋ ㄕㄤ；shòushāng）

VO：to be wounded；to be injured
那隻狗好像受傷了。
That dog seems to be wounded.

2. 麻布（ㄇㄚˊ ㄅㄨˋ；mábù）

N：hemp cloth
以前人常用麻布做成袋子。
In the past, people often used hemp cloth for making bags.

3. 怪（ㄍㄨㄞˋ；guài）

A：very
那個乞丐怪可憐的。
That beggar is very pitiful.

4. 獵人（ㄌㄧㄝˋ ㄖㄣˊ；liè-rén）

N：a hunter

5. 翻臉（ㄈㄢ ㄌㄧㄢˇ；fānliǎn）

IE：to turn hostile；to get angry；to show displeasure
你再這麼大聲對我叫，我就和你翻臉了！
If you shout at me that loudly again, I will become angry with you.

6. 杏樹（ㄒㄧㄥˋ ㄕㄨˋ；shìngshù）

N：an apricot tree

7. 稀奇 (ㄒㄧ ㄑㄧˊ ; shīchí)
   SV：rare；unusual
   熊貓是很稀奇的動物。
   Pandas are very rare animals.

8. 結 (ㄐㄧㄝˊ ; jié)
   FV：to bear fruit
   這棵樹結了很多蘋果。
   This tree bears many apples.

9. 合理 (ㄏㄜˊ ㄌㄧˇ ; hélǐ)
   SV：reasonable；logical
   這個價錢很合理。
   This price is very reasonable.

10. 扔 (ㄖㄥ ; rēng)
    FV：to throw；to hurt
    請不要把東西扔在地上。
    Please don't throw things on the ground.

11. 評判 (ㄆㄧㄥˊ ㄆㄢˋ ; píngpàn)
    FV：to judge or decide (as in a contest)；judgment, etc.

12. 老頭子 (ㄌㄠˇ ㄊㄡˊ ˙ㄗ ; lǎutóutz)
    N：an old man

13. 也許 (ㄧㄝˇ ㄒㄩˇ ; yěshiǔ)
    MA：maybe；perhaps

也許明天會下雨。
Maybe it will rain tomorrow.

14. 調查 (ㄉㄧㄠˋ ㄔㄚˊ ; diàuchá)

FV：to investigate ; to probe ; to survey ; an investigation
你可以幫我調查一下這個人嗎？
Can you help me investigate this person?

15. 憋死 (ㄅㄧㄝ ㄙˇ ; biēsž)

RE：to die from suffocation ; to feel (a situation) is extremely stifling
我每天待在家裡，簡直快憋死了。
I stay at home every day. It's almost suffocating me to death.

16. 紮 (ㄓㄚˊ ; já)

FV：to bind ; to tie ; to fasten

17. 緊 (ㄐㄧㄣˇ ; jǐn)

SV：tight ; firm ; secure ; taut ; tense
這束木柴紮得緊緊的。
The bundle of firewood is tied tightly.

18. 憋氣 (ㄅㄧㄝ ㄑㄧˋ ; biēchì)

VO：to suffer a breathing obstruction ; to hold your breath
他在水裡憋氣憋了好久。
He has held his breath under the water for a long time.

19. 畜生（ㄔㄨˋ ㄕㄥ；chùshēng）
   N：dumb creatures ; cruel animal
   狼根本就是一隻畜生。
   The wolf is basically a cruel animal.

20. 人情（ㄖㄣˊ ㄑㄧㄥˊ；rénchíng）
   N：good will (expressed in the form of gifts, invitations, etc) ; favors asked or done
   我不喜歡欠人家的人情。
   I don't like to owe people favors.

II. 成　語

1. 忘恩負義（ㄨㄤˋ ㄣ ㄈㄨˋ ㄧˋ；wàng-ēnfùyì）
   ungrateful ; ingratitude ; devoid of gratitude.
   人不可忘恩負義。
   People shouldn't be ungrateful.

2. 救人要救到底（ㄐㄧㄡˋ ㄖㄣˊ ㄧㄠˋ ㄐㄧㄡˋ ㄉㄠˋ ㄉㄧˇ；jioùrényàujioudàudǐ）
   When saving somebody, save them completely.
   救人要救到底，不要只救到一半。
   When saving somebody, save them completely. Don't just save them half-way.

3. 没安好心（ㄇㄟˊ ㄢ ㄏㄠˇ ㄒㄧㄣ；méiānhǎushīn）
   to have bad intentions
   那個人對你没安好心。

That person has bad intentions towards you.

4. 誰是誰非（ㄕㄟˊ ㄕˋ ㄕㄟˊ ㄈㄟ；shéishrshéifei）

Who is right and who is wrong

我不喜歡談論誰是誰非。

I don't like to discuss who is right and who is wrong.

是非 right and wrong

5. 無情無義（ㄨˊ ㄑㄧㄥˊ ㄨˊ ㄧˋ；wúchíngwúyì）

heartless and ruthless

他是個無情無義的人。

He is a heartless and ruthless person.

III. 練　習

1. 用下列詞語造句：

　　1)可憐的

　　2)躲

　　3)解開

　　4)反而

　　5)砍

　　6)最後

　　7)卻

　　8)也許

　　9)就是

　　10)這樣子

2. 回答下列問題：

1) 東郭先生為什麼要救那隻狼呢？
2) 東郭先生為什麼要對獵人說謊呢？
3) 狼翻了臉，要把東郭先生吃了；東郭先生怎麼說？
4) 狼又怎麼說？
5) 老杏樹認為狼吃東郭先生合理嗎？為什麼？
6) 老牛為什麼不幫助東郭先生？
7) 老頭子為什麼說：狼吃東郭先生，也許是有道理？
8) 老頭子叫狼自己鑽進袋子裡，是為什麼？
9) 你認為老杏樹、老牛、老頭子，那一個說的話比較有道理？
10) 你認為東郭先生會殺死狼嗎？

第十四課　不合時宜的詩人

　　蘇東坡是宋朝最多才多藝的文人，不但詩、詞、散文寫的非常好，就是寫的字，畫的竹子也非常有名。

　　一〇八九年，他出任杭州太守；西湖就是他在杭州時候所開發成為中國有名的風景區的。湖上有一道長堤，就叫「蘇公堤」；堤上建有六座橋樑，兩旁種有桃花、柳樹。他自己還寫了一首讚美西湖的詩：
「水光瀲灧晴方好，山色空濛雨亦奇；
欲把西湖比西子，淡粧濃抹總相宜。」

　　他的朋友郭公甫，有一次來拜訪他，兩人談得很高興。郭公甫就拿出他最近寫的一首詩，給東坡看，並且自己吟唱了起來，聲調很優美。吟唱完了，問說；「我這首詩，可

— 159 —

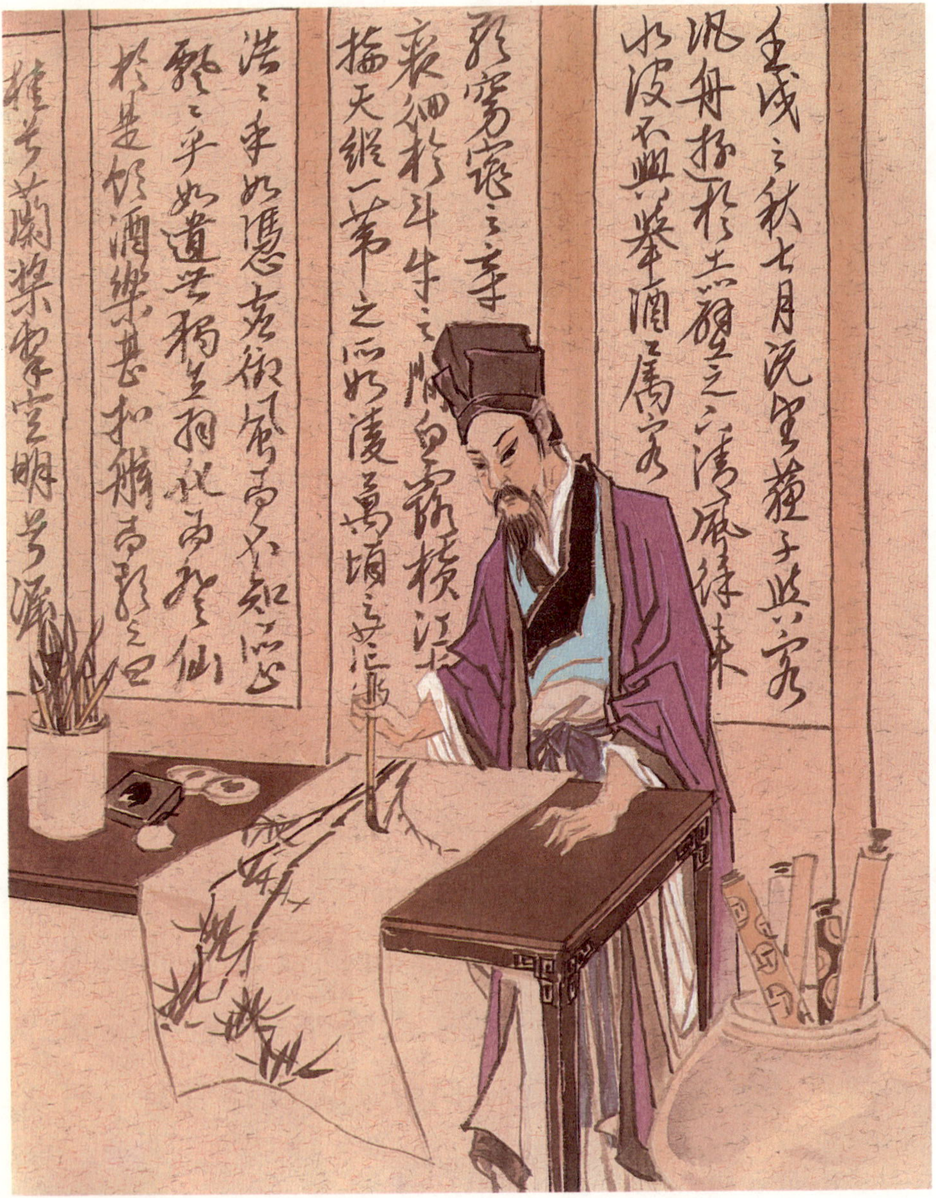

以打幾分？」東坡說：「十分。」

郭公甫聽了十分歡喜，又問：「爲什麼可以打十分呢？」

東坡說：「七分是吟唱，三分是詩篇；合起來，豈不是十分！」一句話就使郭公甫由十分歡喜，變成了十分失望。蘇東坡就是這樣的一個直腸子的人。

王安石研究文字，寫了一本「字說」，請東坡表示一些意見。東坡說：「我的號『東坡』；這個『坡』字，怎麼講呢？」王安石說：「『坡』的意思，就是『土』的『皮』。」東坡不贊同王安石的解釋，又直率地反駁說：「那麼『滑』字，就是『水』的『骨』嗎？」

東坡也知道自己說話太直率的缺點，常常會得罪朋友。有一次，他吃過了晚飯，覺得有點飽，就摸著自己的腹部，對家人說：「你們說：我這裡面裝的是什麼東西？」有一個人說：「都是文章啊！」東坡不以爲然，又一個

說:「滿腹都是『機智[50]』。」東坡仍然不認為說的很對,又問朝雲[51]。她就說:「先生是一肚子的『不合時宜』。」東坡就捧腹大笑了起來。

I. 生字與生詞

1. 宋朝（ㄙㄨㄥˋ ㄔㄠˊ；sùngcháu）
   N：The Sùng Dynasty (960-1279 A.D.)

2. 文人（ㄨㄣˊ ㄖㄣˊ；wénrén）
   N：a man of letters

3. 詩（ㄕ；shr̄）
   N：poem; poetry

4. 詞（ㄘˊ；tsź）
   N：a form of poetry characterized by lines of irregular length which reached its zenith in the Sùng Dynasty（宋朝）

5. 散文（ㄙㄢˇ ㄨㄣˊ；sǎnwén）
   N：prose; essays

6. 竹子（ㄓㄨˊ ˙ㄗ；jútz）
   N：bamboo

7. 出任（ㄔㄨ ㄖㄣˋ；chūrèn）
   FV：to assume a position; to take office
   你認為誰會出任下一屆總統？
   Who do you think will be the next president?

8. 杭州（ㄏㄤˊ ㄓㄡ；hángjōu）

N：Háng-jōu is situated in Jè-jiāng Province（浙江省）.

9. 太守（ㄊㄞˋ ㄕㄡˇ；tàishǒu）

   N：warden; magistrate (governor) of a prefecture.

10. 西湖（ㄒㄧ ㄏㄨˊ；shīhú）

    N：the West Lake, a well-known scenic and historical area in Háng-jōu

11. 開發（ㄎㄞ ㄈㄚ；kāifā）

    FV：to develop; developed; development (of natural resources; industry, etc.)
    這個國家正在開發中。
    This country is developing.

12. 風景區（ㄈㄥ ㄐㄧㄥˇ ㄑㄩ；fēngjǐngchiū）

    N：scenic area
    西湖是中國最有名的風景區之一。
    The West Lake is one of China's most famous scenic areas.
    區　N：an area, district or zone

13. 長堤（ㄔㄤˊ ㄊㄧ；chángtí）

    N：a long dike

14. 蘇公堤（ㄙㄨ ㄍㄨㄥ ㄊㄧ；sūgūngtí）

    N：the name of the dike built on The West Lake（西湖）by Sū Dūng-pō（蘇東坡）, when he was magistrate for Háng-jōu（杭州）
    公　N：a respectful term of address

第十四課　不合時宜的詩人　165

15. 橋樑（ㄑㄧㄠˊ ㄌㄧㄤˊ；chiáuliáng）
    N：a bridge

16. 桃花（ㄊㄠˊ ㄏㄨㄚ；táuhuā）
    N：the peach blossom (often used to symbolize Spring)
    春天是桃花盛開的季節。
    Spring is the season when peach blossoms are in full bloom.

17. 柳樹（ㄌㄧㄡˇ ㄕㄨˋ；liǒushù）
    N：the willow tree

18. 首（ㄕㄡˇ；shǒu）
    M：measure word for poems, songs, etc.
    請你為我們唱一首歌好嗎？
    Please sing a song for us, OK?

19. 讚美（ㄗㄢˋ ㄇㄟˇ；tzànměi）
    FV：to praise; to glorify; to exalt
    誰不喜歡聽人家讚美呢？
    Who doesn't like to hear the praise of others?

20. 瀲灩（ㄌㄧㄢˋ ㄧㄢˋ；liànyàn）
    SV：the movement and flowing of water

21. 晴方好（ㄑㄧㄥˊ ㄈㄤ ㄏㄠˇ；chíngfānghǎu）
    IE：perfectly clear and sunny

22. 空濛（ㄎㄨㄥ ㄇㄥˊ；kūngméng）
    SV：the misty atmosphere of rainy days

23. 亦（ㄧˋ；yì）
    A：likewise；also, as well
    相見時難別亦難。
    To meet is difficult；likewise to part.

24. 奇（ㄑㄧˊ；chí）
    SV：rare；special；wonderful

25. 欲（ㄩˋ；yù）
    FV：to want to；to desire to

26. 西子（ㄒㄧ ㄗˇ；shītž）
    N：a famous beauty of the Spring and Autumn Period；sometimes called Shī Shī（西施）
    西子是中國四大美人之一。
    Shī Tž is one of the "four beauties" of China.

27. 淡粧濃抹（ㄉㄢˋ ㄓㄨㄤ ㄋㄨㄥˊ ㄇㄛˇ；dànjuāng núngmǒ）
    IE：heavy or light makeup

28. 相宜（ㄒㄧㄤ ㄧˊ；shiāngyí）
    SV：suitable；fitting.

29. 郭公甫（ㄍㄨㄛ ㄍㄨㄥ ㄈㄨˇ；guōgūngfǔ）

N：a friend of Sū Dūng-pō

30. 吟唱（ㄧㄣˊ ㄔㄤˋ；yínchàng）

FV：to recite and sing

31. 聲調（ㄕㄥ ㄉㄧㄠˋ；shēngdiàu）

N：the tone of a voice
她唱歌的聲調優美極了。
The tone of her singing is really beautiful.

32. 打（ㄉㄚˇ；dǎ）

V：to give (a grade, discount, etc)
這篇文章老師給你打幾分？
What grade did the teacher give you for this composition?

33. 詩篇（ㄕ ㄆㄧㄢ；shrpiān）

N：poem
篇　M：measure word for poems, compositions, etc.

34. 豈不是（ㄑㄧˇ ㄅㄨˋ ㄕˋ；chǐbúshr̀）

A：How could it not be；wouldn't that be
他偷了人家的東西，豈不是要被判刑？
He stole people's things. How couldn't he be sentenced?

35. 直腸子（ㄓˊ ㄔㄤˊ ˙ㄗ；jŕchángtz）

IE：outspoken；frank；blunt
他是個直腸子，有什麼說什麼。
He is very frank. He says what he thinks.

36. 王安石（ㄨㄤˊ ㄢ ㄕˊ；wángānshŕ）

 N：A statesman and contemporary of Sū Dūng-pō who advocated government and law reform.

37. 字說（ㄗˋ ㄕㄨㄛ；tzshuō）

 N："Characters Explained", the title of a book explaining characters

38. 號（ㄏㄠˋ；hàu）

 N：second name

39. 贊同（ㄗㄢˋ ㄊㄨㄥˊ；tzàntúng）

 FV：to approve of；to consent to；to agree with
 我不贊同你的意見。
 I don't agree with your opinion.

40. 直率（ㄓˊ ㄕㄨㄞˋ；jŕshuài）

 SV：direct；frank；honest；blunt
 他是個很直率的人。
 He is a very direct person.

41. 反駁（ㄈㄢˇ ㄅㄛˊ；fǎnbó）

 FV：to refute；to rebut；to dispute
 我已經知道事情的真相了，你不要再反駁了。
 I already know the truth of the matter. You needn't continue disputing it.

42. 滑（ㄏㄨㄚˊ；huá）

SV：to slip；to slide；slippery；cunning；insincere

43. **缺點**（ㄑㄩㄝ ㄉㄧㄢˇ；chiuēdiǎn）

    N：shortcoming；defect；flaw
    每個人都有缺點。
    Everyone has shortcomings.

44. **得罪**（ㄉㄜˊ ㄗㄨㄟˋ；détzuèi）

    FV：to offend
    他說話太坦率，所以常常得罪朋友。
    He talks too directly, and so often offends his friends.

45. **飽**（ㄅㄠˇ；bǎu）

    SV：to be full (stomach)
    我總覺得吃不飽。
    I never feel full.

46. **摸**（ㄇㄛ；mō）

    FV：to feel or touch (with the fingers)
    有時候，我真希望能摸到天空的雲。
    Sometimes, I really wish I could touch the clouds in the sky.

47. **腹部**（ㄈㄨˋ ㄅㄨˋ；fùbù）

    N：the belly；the abdomen
    腹部是在人體胸部的下面。
    The abdomen is below the chest of the body.

48. **裝**（ㄓㄨㄤ；juāng）

FV：to pack ; to fill in or up
請你把書裝在盒子裡，好不好？
Please pack the books in the box, OK?

49. 文章（ㄨㄣˊ ㄓㄤ ; wénjāng）

N：writing ; composition
她的文章寫得很好。
Her composition is written very well.

50. 機智（ㄐㄧ ㄓˋ ; jījr）

N：alertness ; wit ; ready responsiveness
他的話裡充滿了機智。
His words are full of wit.

51. 朝雲（ㄓㄠ ㄩㄣˊ ; jāuyún）

N：the name of a concubine of Sū Dūng-pō.

II. 成 語

1. 不合時宜（ㄅㄨˋ ㄏㄜˊ ㄕˊ ㄧˊ ; bùhéshŕyí）

be out of keeping with the times ; be incompatible with present needs. ; be out of keeping with the objective conditions

2. 不以爲然（ㄅㄨˋ ㄧˇ ㄨㄟˊ ㄖㄢˊ ; bùjǐwéirán）

object to ; not approve ; it take exception to…
他認爲中文很難，我不以爲然。
He thinks Chinese is difficult. I don't think so.

3. 捧腹大笑（ㄆㄥˇ ㄈㄨˋ ㄉㄚˋ ㄒㄧㄠˋ; pěngfùdàshiàu）
to split (hold) one's sides with laughter
我的笑話令我媽媽捧腹大笑。
My joke made my mother hold her sides with laughter.

III. 練　習

1. 用下列詞語造句：

　　1)出任
　　2)開發
　　3)兩旁
　　4)山色
　　5)淡粧
　　6)拜訪
　　7)並且
　　8)吟唱
　　9) 打
　　10)得罪

2. 回答下列問題：

　　1)爲什麼說，蘇東坡是個多才多藝的文人？
　　2)蘇東坡曾經做什麼官職？做了那些事？
　　3)蘇東坡對杭州西湖寫了一首詩，你能不能背誦出來？
　　4)試舉一個例子，說明蘇東坡率直的個性。

5)王安石也是有名的文人,他研究什麼呢?
6)王安石對東坡的「坡」字,作何解釋?
7)蘇東坡對王安石的解釋,滿意嗎?
8)蘇東坡自己知道直率會得罪朋友嗎?
9)爲什麼蘇東坡聽見朝雲說他「不合時宜」就捧腹大笑?
10)你認爲蘇東坡的肚子裡裝的是什麼呢?

第十五課　小魚的快樂

莊子是戰國時代有名的哲學家。他認為人所要過的就是自由自在、適合本性的生活。有一天夜裡，他夢見自己變成了一隻翩翩飛舞的蝴蝶。他從夢裡驚醒時說：「到底是我變成了蝴蝶，還是蝴蝶此刻變成了我呢？人生真的只是一場美麗的夢！」他認為人由誕生到死亡，由年輕到衰老，就像春夏秋冬四季的變化，都是屬於自然的現象，所以我們不必為生高興，為死悲傷！

莊子不只是一個很有思想的人，而且口才也很好。

有一天，他和朋友惠施，到郊外散步。這時，天氣漸漸暖和，到處開滿花朵，黃鶯在柳枝上唱歌，農夫在田裡插秧。他們看到這

中國寓言故事

樣美麗的春光，心裡十分高興，慢慢走到水邊，走到橋上。往下看，突然有一群小魚兒，從石縫裡輕快地游了過來。莊子看了，笑著說：「老惠，快來看，這些可愛的小魚兒！」他覺得牠們游得那麼逍遙自在，而人的生活卻是那麼忙碌緊張，因此說：「你看這些魚，多麼快樂呀！」惠施有意要難倒莊子，就說：「你又不是魚，怎麼知道魚的快樂呢？」

但是他卻沒想到，莊子就用他的話回答他，說：「你又不是我，又怎麼知道我不知道魚的快樂呀？」說得惠施啞口無言。這時，莊子就哈哈大笑起來。

I. 生字與生詞

1. 莊子 (ㄓㄨㄤ ㄗˇ ; juāngtž)

    N：姓莊名周 (ㄓㄡ ; Jōu) Famous Philosopher of the Warring States Period

2. 本性 (ㄅㄣˇ ㄒㄧㄥˋ ; běnshìng)

    N：the real nature ; natural character
    人的本性是善良的。
    People are good natured.

3. 蝴蝶 (ㄏㄨˊ ㄉㄧㄝˊ ; húdié)

    N：butterfly

4. 此刻 (ㄘˇ ㄎㄜˋ ; tsžkè)

    N：at this moment
    我真希望此刻下大雨。
    I really hope that it will start to rain right now.

5. 誕生 (ㄉㄢˋ ㄕㄥ ; dànshēng)

    FV：be born
    N：birth
    孫逸仙的誕生對中國有很重大的意義。
    Sun Yat-sen's birth is of great significance to China.

6. 四季 (ㄙˋ ㄐㄧˋ ; szjì)

    N：the four seasons
    台灣的四季不很明顯。

Taiwan's four seasons are not very distinct.

7. 屬於（ㄕㄨˇ ㄩˊ；shǔyú）

   FV：to belong to
   這輛車子是屬於誰的？
   To whom does this car belong?

8. 思想（ㄙ ㄒㄧㄤˇ；szshiǎng）

   N：thoughts；ideas；thinking
   他的思想很開放。
   His thinking is very liberal.

9. 口才（ㄎㄡˇ ㄘㄞˊ；kǒutsái）

   N：eloquence
   我爸爸的口才很好。
   My father is very eloquent.

10. 惠施（ㄏㄨㄟˋ ㄕ；hùeishr̄）

    N：Hùei Shr̄, a good friend of Juāng Tž（莊子）。

11. 散步（ㄙㄢˋ ㄅㄨˋ；sànbù）

    FV：a stroll；to take a walk
    這個周末，我想去郊外散步。
    This weekend, I would like to go to the suburbs for a stroll.

12. 到處（ㄉㄠˋ ㄔㄨˋ；dàuchù）

    N：everywhere；all places
    夏天的海邊，到處是人。

The beach in summer is covered with people everywhere.

13. 花朵（ㄏㄨㄚ ㄉㄨㄛˇ；huāduǒ）
    N：flowers

14. 黃鶯（ㄏㄨㄤˊ ㄧㄥ；huángyīng）
    N：oriole(s)

15. 農夫（ㄋㄨㄥˊ ㄈㄨ；núngfū）
    N：farmer(s)
    現在很少人想當農夫。
    Nowadays very few people want to be farmers.

16. 插秧（ㄔㄚ ㄧㄤ；chāyāng）
    VO：transplanting rice seedlings
    農夫在春天辛苦地插秧。
    Farmers at springtime laboriously transplant rice seedlings.
    插　FV：to insert；to plant

17. 石縫（ㄕˊ ㄈㄥˋ；shŕfèng）
    N：a crevice between rocks or in a rock
    這個石縫中長了很多野草。
    This rock crevice has a lot of wild grass growing in it.
    縫　B：a crack；an opening；a fissure

18. 輕快（ㄑㄧㄥ ㄎㄨㄞˋ；chīngkuài）
    SV：sprightly；lightly；agile；brisk；lively
    那是一首很輕快的歌。

That is a brisk and lively song.

19. 逍遙自在（ㄒㄧㄠ ㄧㄠˊ ㄗˋ ㄗㄞˋ；shiāuyáutzìtzài）

    IE：to enjoy an unrestrained, happy and leisurely life；carefree
    他的生活過得很逍遙自在。
    He lives happily and carefree.

20. 忙碌（ㄇㄤˊ ㄌㄨˋ；mánglù）

    SV：busy and in great haste；be fully occupied
    她的工作很忙碌。
    She is very busy in her job.

21. 緊張（ㄐㄧㄣˇ ㄓㄤ；Jǐnjāng）

    SV：tense；nervous
    不要緊張，慢慢來。
    Relax, take it easy.

22. 有意（地）（ㄧㄡˇ ㄧˋ；yǒuyì）

    A：intentionally
    我不是有意傷害你的感情。
    I didn't mean to hurt your feelings.

23. 難倒（ㄋㄢˊ ㄉㄠˇ；nándǎu）

    to baffle；be baffled
    to put (somebody) into a situation where they can't answer a question, solve a problem, etc.
    你把我難倒了。
    You have got me.

II. 成語

1. **自由自在** (ㄗˋ ㄧㄡˊ ㄗˋ ㄗㄞˋ; tzỳyóutzỳtzài)

    carefree; comfortable and at ease
    我喜歡一個人自由自在地過日子。
    I like to pass the days carefree and alone.

2. **翩翩飛舞** (ㄆㄧㄢ ㄆㄧㄢ ㄈㄟ ㄨˇ; piānpiānfēiwǔ)

    to fly gracefully and lightly
    她的舞姿優美，就像翩翩飛舞的蝴蝶。
    Her dancing is beautiful, just like a gracefully flying butterfly.

3. **不必爲生高興，爲死悲傷** (ㄅㄨˊ ㄅㄧˋ ㄨㄟˋ ㄕㄥ ㄍㄠ ㄒㄧㄥˋ, ㄨㄟˋ ㄙˇ ㄅㄟ ㄕㄤ; búbìwèishēnggāushìng, wèisž̌bēishāng)

    It's not necessary to be happy because of life, or sad because of death (ie, life and death are natural)
    莊子認爲我們不必爲生高興，爲死悲傷。
    Juāng Tž reckons it is not necessary to be happy because of life or sad because of death.

4. **啞口無言** (ㄧㄚˇ ㄎㄡˇ ㄨˊ ㄧㄢˊ; yǎkǒuwúyán)

    to be speechless (unable to reply to a question, having one's argument completely demolished, etc)
    他問得我啞口無言。
    His questioning left me speechless.

III. 詞組與句型

1. 到底是…，還是 to really be…, or not be

這個可愛的小孩到底是男生，還是女生？
Is this cute child really a boy or a girl?
你到底是來，還是不來？
Are you coming or not?

2. 由…到 from…to

由你家到學校有多遠？
How far is it from your house to school?
由唐代到宋代，中國文壇上，出現了很多偉大的文人。
From the Táng Dynasty to the Sùng Dynasty, many great writers appeared on the Chinese literary area.

IV. 練　習

1. 用下列詞語造句：

　　1) 飛
　　2) 游
　　3) 春光
　　4) 還是
　　5) 誕生
　　6) 死亡
　　7) 自然
　　8) 逍遙

9）没想到

10)不只是

2. 回答下列問題：

1)莊子提倡什麼思想？
2)莊子做了什麼夢？
3)到底是莊子變成蝴蝶？還是蝴蝶變成莊子？
4)人生真只是一場美麗的夢嗎？
5)生和死都是自然的現象嗎？
6)莊子在郊外散步，看見什麼？
7)莊子認爲小魚兒很快樂，惠施呢？
8)莊子用什麼說法來回答惠施？
9)你認爲惠施還可以用什麼詭辯方式，來回答莊子？
10)莊子的思想，你贊成嗎？

第十六課　知音難求

　　俞伯牙的七絃琴彈得非常感人。他的朋友鍾子期對音樂的鑑賞力非常高明,能夠聽出演奏者在琴聲中,所寄託的情思。

　　有一天,伯牙焚香彈琴。他忽然想起有一次在泰山遇到下雨,躲進一個山洞裡避雨的情景。雨滴滴答答地落著,真美呀!想到這裡,他隨手彈出一支淋雨曲,非常輕快奔放。鍾子期說:「你彈得真好哇!好像湯湯的流水!」伯牙又想起當時雨越下越大,閃電打雷,天色昏暗,傾盆大雨遮沒了山下綠綠的梯田,峭壁掛下許多道瀑布,好像千丈的銀河倒瀉。伯牙的手指重重地敲擊著琴絃,聲音隨著激昂飛揚起來。伯牙快速有力的琴音,激越雄壯的調子,敲擊著鍾子期的心靈,他說:「彈得好極

184 中國寓言故事

了，好像巍巍高山的飛瀑！」

　　鍾子期成了伯牙的知音。大凡一個詩人、作家、音樂家、畫家創作了作品，都希望有人欣賞他，讚美他；這樣心裡就得到安慰跟鼓勵。

　　後來鍾子期病死了；伯牙到他的墳墓前，彈了一支曲子，祭奠鍾子期之後就把琴摔碎了，說：「子期不在了，我還對誰彈琴呢！雖然我的朋友很多，但是要想找一個知音，能夠瞭解我、欣賞我的朋友，卻是非常困難的！」

Ⅰ. 生字與生詞

1. **俞伯牙** (ㄩˊ ㄅㄛˊ ㄧㄚˊ；yúbóyá)

    N：Yú Bó-yá, a musician of the Spring and Autumn Period

2. **七絃琴** (ㄑㄧ ㄒㄧㄢˊ ㄑㄧㄣˊ；chīshiánchín)

    N：a seven-stringed Chinese musical instrument
    絃　N：a cord, the string of a musical instrument
    琴　N：a musical instrument (usually stringed)

3. **彈** (ㄊㄢˊ；tán)

    FV：to play (a piano or a stringed instrument)
    你會不會彈七絃琴？
    Can you play the chī shián chín?

4. **感人** (ㄍㄢˇ ㄖㄣˊ；gǎnrén)

    SV：moving；touching
    她的故事很感人。
    Her story is very moving.

5. **鍾子期** (ㄓㄨㄥ ㄗˇ ㄑㄧˊ；jūngtzchí)

    N：Jūng Tz-chí, a friend of Yú Bó-yá and a music lover

6. **鑑賞力** (ㄐㄧㄢˋ ㄕㄤˇ ㄌㄧˋ；jiànshǎnglì)

    N：powers of discernment and appreciation (as a connoisseur might have)
    他對音樂很有鑑賞力。
    He is a connoisseur in music.

7. 高明（ㄍㄠ ㄇㄧㄥˊ; gāuming）

    SV：clever; wise; superior
    他有時候做事的方法很高明。
    Sometimes the way he does things is very clever.

8. 演奏（ㄧㄢˇ ㄗㄡˋ; yǎntzòu）

    FV：(of musicians) to perform
    下個禮拜，他要在很多人的面前演奏鋼琴。
    Next week, he will perform on the piano in front of many people.

9. 寄託（ㄐㄧˋ ㄊㄨㄛ; jìtuō）

    FV：to consign or commit (emotions to writing, soul to god, etc)
    我媽把所有的希望都寄託在我身上。
    My mother has placed all her hopes on me.
    託　FV：to entrust to

10. 焚香（ㄈㄣˊ ㄒㄧㄤ; fénshiāng）

    VO：to burn incense (in worship, offering, etc)
    她每天早上都焚香拜佛。
    Every morning she burns incense worshipping Buddha.

11. 泰山（ㄊㄞˋ ㄕㄢ; tàishān）

    N：Tài Shān, located in Shān-dūng Province（山東省），one of the Five Sacred Mountains.

12. 滴滴答答（ㄉㄧ ㄉㄧ ㄉㄚ ㄉㄚ; dīdīdādā）

ON：the pitter-patter of rain
雨滴滴答答地下著。
The rain pitter-pattered down.

13. 支（ㄓ；jr）

M：measure word for songs, incense；cigarettes；etc

14. 淋雨（ㄌㄧㄣˊ ㄩˇ；línyǔ）

IE：to get wet in the rain
我不喜歡淋雨。
I don't like to get wet in the rain.

15. 曲（ㄑㄩˇ；chiǔ）

N & M：a piece of music；measure word for a piece of music
那首曲子很美。
That piece of music is very beautiful.

16. 奔放（ㄅㄣ ㄈㄤˋ；bēnfàng）

SV：(said of writing, emotions, etc) expressive and unrestrained；moving and forceful
她的個性很奔放。
She has a vigorous and unfettered personality.

17. 湯湯（ㄕㄤ ㄕㄤ；shāngshāng）

SV：(water) flowing turbulently
(of current) rushing

18. 昏暗（ㄏㄨㄣ ㄢˋ；huēnàn）

SV：dark；murky；hazy
天色有點昏暗，看起來好像快下雨了。
It's dark, it looks like it'll rain soon.

19. 遮沒（ㄓㄜ ㄇㄛˋ；jēmò）

FV：to completely cover；to obscure

20. 梯田（ㄊㄧ ㄊㄧㄢˊ；tītián）

N：rice terraces
大雨遮沒了山下的梯田。
The heavy rain completely covered the rice terraces under the mountain.

21. 峭壁（ㄑㄧㄠˋ ㄅㄧˋ；chiàubì）

N：a vertical cliff；a precipice
那座山有很多峭壁。
That mountain has many precipices.

22. 掛（ㄍㄨㄚˋ；guà）

FV：to hang；to suspend
麻煩你把我的大衣掛起來。
Could you please hang up my coat.

23. 瀑布（ㄆㄨˋ ㄅㄨˋ；pùbù）

N：waterfall

24. 敲擊（ㄑㄧㄠ ㄐㄧˊ；chiāují）

FV：to beat；to knock
他用筷子敲擊桌子。

He knocked on the table with chopsticks.

25. 激昂（ㄐㄧ ㄤˊ；jī-áng）
    SV：high-spirited；tremendously excited

26. 飛揚（ㄈㄟ ㄧㄤˊ；fēiyáng）
    FV：to rise up and flutter（as a flag）；to fly about
    我喜歡看她的長髮飛揚在風中。
    I like to watch her long hair blowing in the wind.

27. 激越（ㄐㄧ ㄩㄝˋ；jīyuè）
    SV：sonorous；having a full, rich and deep sound

28. 雄壯（ㄒㄩㄥˊ ㄓㄨㄤˋ；shiúngjuàng）
    SV：powerful；strong；virile；martial
    軍歌通常都很雄壯激昂。
    Military songs are usually powerful and high-spirited.

29. 調子（ㄉㄧㄠˋ ˙ㄗ；diàutz）
    N：a tune；a melody
    這首歌的調子很好聽。
    This song's tune sounds good.

30. 心靈（ㄒㄧㄣ ㄌㄧㄥˊ；shīnlíng）
    N：mind；spirit；spiritual；mental
    不要常打小孩，否則很容易傷害他們幼小的心靈。
    Don't hit children often, otherwise their young spirit will be easily damaged.

31. 巍巍（ㄨㄟˊ ㄨㄟˊ；wéiwéi）
    SV：lofty；majestic；imposing
    那些巍巍的高山看起來很雄壯。
    Those majestic high mountains look magnificent.

32. 知音（ㄓ ㄧㄣ；jryin）
    IE：a close friend who really understands you
    我有很多朋友，卻一個知音也沒有。
    I have many friends, but not one who really understands me.

33. 大凡（ㄉㄚˋ ㄈㄢˊ；dàfán）
    A：generally speaking；ordinarily
    大凡在年輕時肯努力的人，都能擁有成功的事業。
    Generally people who are willing to work hard when (they are) young, will have a successful career.

34. 作家（ㄗㄨㄛˋ ㄐㄧㄚ；tzuòjiā）
    N：writer

35. 創作（ㄔㄨㄤˋ ㄗㄨㄛˋ；chuàngtzuò）
    FV：to create (an original work of literature or art)
    N：an original work of literature or art
    他的創作能力很高。
    His creative abilities are immense.

36. 安慰（ㄢ ㄨㄟˋ；ānwèi）
    FV：to console；to comfort；to soothe

他似乎受了很大的傷害，你應該去安慰他。
He seems to be deeply hurt. You should go and comfort him.

37. 鼓勵（ㄍㄨˇ ㄌㄧˋ；gǔlì）

FV：to encourage；encouragement
我鼓勵你去學日文，因爲你的語言能力很強。
I encourage you to study Japanese because your ability in languages is very strong.

38. 祭奠（ㄐㄧˋ ㄉㄧㄢˋ；jìdiàn）

FV：to offer sacrifices to the spirit of a deceased person
大部分的人用鮮花來祭奠死去的朋友。
Most people use fresh flowers to offer to the deceased friends.

II. 成　語

1. 知音難求（ㄓ ㄧㄣ ㄋㄢˊ ㄑㄧㄡˊ；jṟyīnnánchióu）

a bosom friend keenly appreciative of your talent is hard to find
朋友到處都可以找到，可是知音難求。
Friends can be found everywhere, but who can really understand you is hard to find.

2. 閃電打雷（ㄕㄢˇ ㄉㄧㄢˋ ㄉㄚˇ ㄌㄟˊ；shǎndiàndǎléi）

lightning and thunder
閃電打雷之後，通常會有一場大雨。
After lightning and thunder, there will usually be heavy

rain.

3. 傾盆大雨（ㄑㄧㄥ ㄆㄣˊ ㄉㄚˋ ㄩˇ；chīngpéndàyǔ）
   heavy rain；pouring
   昨晚下了一場傾盆大雨。
   Last night there was heavy rain.

4. 銀河倒瀉（ㄧㄣˊ ㄏㄜˊ ㄉㄠˋ ㄒㄧㄝˋ；yínhédàushiè）
   a silvery stream cascading downward
   山上流下來的瀑布真像銀河倒瀉一般。
   The waterfall falling down from the mountain is really like a cascading silver stream.

III. 練 習

1. 用下列詞語造句：

    1) 能夠
    2) 感人
    3) 寄託
    4) 知音
    5) 遮沒
    6) 摔碎
    7) 瞭解
    8) 欣賞
    9) 流水
    10) 高山

2. 回答下列問題：

　　1) 俞伯牙彈的是什麼琴？
　　2) 俞伯牙爲什麼先焚香後彈琴？
　　3) 俞伯牙遇到下雨，聽到山泉聲；他用什麼琴音來表現？
　　4) 後來雨越下越大，伯牙又怎麼去表現呢？
　　5) 雨傾盆倒下，成千丈的銀河倒瀉，伯牙又如何表現呢？
　　6) 鍾子期可以聽出伯牙的琴音的內容嗎？？
　　7) 爲什麼伯牙要在鍾子期墳墓前彈奏一曲？
　　8) 伯牙摔碎七絃琴，爲了什麼？
　　9) 你也有知音的朋友嗎？
　10) 你有對牛彈琴的經驗嗎？

第十七課　替貓取別號

　　李家養了一隻黃貓，行動非常敏捷，並且很會捕捉老鼠。每天傍晚，牠總要到處巡視一番，眼珠發著閃閃的綠光，看來好像一隻小老虎。

　　這家主人和他的朋友商量，要給牠取個別號。他說：「我家這隻貓，不像別家的，吃飯有鮮魚，睡覺有地毯，教那些老鼠咬壞圖書、衣服也不管。我的貓一叫，老鼠聽到牠的聲音，就逃竄得無影無蹤；所以我要叫牠做『虎貓』。」

　　他想了一想，覺得老虎雖然威猛，但不如龍的神奇，所以應該叫做「龍貓」。又想，龍固然比老虎神奇，但要飛騰上天，還需要浮雲幫助；這樣看來，雲不是比龍更高一等嗎？

196　中國寓言故事

第十七課　替貓取別號

不如就叫牠「雲貓」。

他又想：陰雲滿天，遮沒了太陽、月亮，但一颳大風，雲一下子就會被吹散，乾脆叫這隻貓做「風貓」。但是他心裏想：颳起大風，風力雖然非常強，牆能擋住風，就叫做「牆貓」吧！

他再想想：牆雖然堅固，但老鼠能夠一點一點的挖牆根鑽洞，使整個牆崩塌。牆碰到老鼠又沒有轍了！就叫牠做「鼠貓」。

他的朋友笑他說：「哎呀，能捕老鼠的，本來就是『貓』。貓就叫『貓』呀，何必故意改什麼名字？而失掉牠的本真！」

Ⅰ. 生字與生詞

1. 貓 (ㄇㄠ ; māu)
   N：cat(s)

2. 捕捉 (ㄅㄨˇ ㄓㄨㄛ ; bǔjuō)
   FV：to catch
   他們昨晚捕捉到一隻老鼠。
   Last night they caught a rat.

3. 老鼠 (ㄌㄠˇ ㄕㄨˇ ; lǎushǔ)
   N：a rat ; a mouse

4. 傍晚 (ㄅㄤ ㄨㄢˇ ; bāngwǎn)
   N：dusk ; twilight
   每到傍晚，我就想去散步。
   Every time dusk comes, I feel like going for a walk.

5. 巡視 (ㄒㄩㄣˊ ㄕˋ ; shiúnshr̀)
   FV：to inspect (usually said of ranking officials)

6. （一）番 (ㄈㄢ ; yifān)
   M：measure word for taking a look, inspecting, thinking, a trip, etc.
   警察每晚都要去街上巡視一番。
   Every night policemen need to go to the street to make a tour of inspection.

7. 地毯（ㄉㄧˋ ㄊㄢˇ；dìtǎn）
   N：a rug；a carpet

8. 教（ㄐㄧㄠˋ；jiàu）
   FV：to let；to make
   你真教我生氣。
   You really make me angry.

9. 咬（ㄧㄠˇ；yǎu）
   FV：to bite；to gnaw
   昨天她被狗咬了。
   She was bitten by a dog yesterday.

10. 圖書（ㄊㄨˊ ㄕㄨ；túshū）
    N：maps, charts and books
    圖書館裡有很多圖書。
    Libraries have many books, maps, etc.

11. 威猛（ㄨㄟ ㄇㄥˇ；wēiměng）
    SV：awe-inspiring；imposing；dignified；majestic；fierce；violent
    老虎看起來很威猛。
    Tigers look fierce and awe-inspiring.

12. 龍（ㄌㄨㄥˊ；lúng）
    N：dragon

13. 神奇（ㄕㄣˊ ㄑㄧˊ；shén chí）

SV：mysterious；wondrous；marvelous
愛情是一種很神奇的感情。
Love is a wondrous feeling.

14. 飛騰（ㄈㄟ ㄊㄥˊ；fēiténg）

FV：to fly high
海裡的浪花，有時候好像千萬匹白馬在飛騰。
Sometimes sea spray seems like millions of flying white horses.

15. 浮雲（ㄈㄨˊ ㄩㄣˊ；fúyún）

N：floating cloud
有時候，他看著天上的浮雲發呆。
Sometimes, in a daze, he watches the clouds floating in the sky.
浮　FV：to float

16. 陰雲（ㄧㄣ ㄩㄣˊ；yīnyún）

N：dark clouds

17. 颳（ㄍㄨㄚ；guā）

FV：to blow
不論風颳得多大，我都會去學校。
No matter how hard the wind blows, I always go to school.

18. 擋住（ㄉㄤˇ ㄓㄨˋ；dǎngjù）

FV：to block；to obstruct；to impede
天上的黑雲擋住了太陽。
The dark clouds in the sky shut off the sun.

19. 崩塌（ㄅㄥ ㄊㄚ；bēngtā）

FV：to collapse
他家的牆昨晚崩塌了。
His wall collapsed last night.

20. 碰到（ㄆㄥˋ ㄉㄠˋ；pèngdàu）

RC：to meet someone unexpectedly；to touch something
我昨天在路上碰到一個老朋友。
Last night I bumped into an old friend on the street.

21. 沒轍（ㄇㄟˊ ㄓㄜˊ；méijé）

VO：no way or method (to do something)
我妹妹平常很會說話，但一碰到我爸爸，她就沒轍了。
Usually my sister really knows how to talk；but, as soon as she encounters my father she's at a loss.

22. 故意（ㄍㄨˋ ㄧˋ；gùyì）

A：on purpose；intentionally
對不起，我不是故意要傷害你的。
I'm sorry, I didn't mean to hurt you.

23. 失掉（ㄕ ㄉㄧㄠˋ；shīdiàu）

FV：to lose (a chance, faith, confidence, courage, etc)

24. 本真（ㄅㄣˇ ㄓㄣ；běnjēn）

N：real self；the real look
不管別人怎麼笑你，你都不要改變自己而失掉你的本真。
No matter how others laugh at you, don't ever change

yourself and lose your real self.
SV：single and sincere

II. 成　語

1. 逃竄無蹤（ㄊㄠˊ ㄘㄨㄢˋ ㄨˊ ㄗㄨㄥ；táutsuàn-wútzūng）

    to disperse and flee, leaving no trace
    老鼠一看到貓，就逃竄無蹤了。
    As soon as mice see a cat, they flee without trace.
    蹤　N：trace；track

2. 更高一等（ㄍㄥˋ ㄍㄠ ㄧˋ ㄉㄥˇ；gènggāu-yīděng）

    even better
    我的數學很好，但是他的比我的更高一等。
    My mathematics is very good, but his is even better than mine.

III. 練　習

1. 用下列詞語造句：

    1) 敏捷
    2) 雖然
    3) 比
    4) 叫做
    5) 非常

6) 不如
7) 就
8) 挖
9) 鑽
10) 崩塌

2. 回答下列問題：

1) 李家的貓長相如何？
2) 李家如何飼養這隻黃貓？
3) 李家的貓爲什麼叫「虎貓」？
4) 又爲什麼叫「龍貓」？
5) 取名「龍貓」，爲什麼又改名「雲貓」？
6) 「雲貓」敵得過「風貓」嗎？
7) 「風貓」爲什麼又不如「牆貓」呢？
8) 「牆貓」爲什麼又不如叫「貓」呢？
9) 貓抓老鼠的本領是不是天生的？
10) 最後，李家的這隻貓有沒有改成牠的名字？

第十八課　狗和稻子

　　原始時代，野草灌木叢生，毒蛇猛獸成群，人類的生活非常艱苦。

　　有一天，玉皇大帝召開天神會議。他說：「幾千萬年前，我們創造了大地，讓大地長出許多花草樹木，生出許多飛鳥走獸游魚昆蟲，使大地充滿著蓬勃的生命，猛烈的競爭，但也使人類驚擾恐懼，因為要跟各種動物搏鬥，爭奪有限的食物。這個實在違反了我們創造萬物的原意。我們原本希望人類和萬物能夠和平相處；現在，他們卻不斷的為爭奪食物而相互屠殺。」

　　「萬神的大帝，你真是太慈悲了。」盤古說：「我們創造動物的時候，給了牠們利爪、尖牙、長角、大翼；同樣的，我們給了

206 中國寓言故事

人類智慧的頭腦、靈巧的雙手、能直立走路的兩腳。人類有這些特別的能力，應該足夠利用萬物維持生命、繁衍種族的。」

「你說的雖然不錯。」神農說：「但人類不知節育，人口不斷增加；專靠捕魚、打獵，是不夠吃的。」

「神農，」玉皇大帝說：「你可有什麼好辦法，來解決這個問題？」

「我們可以教人類種水稻呀！這樣就可以大量生產糧食了。」

「除了送水稻去，還應該給人類一些動物做幫手。」神農又說：「老虎、獅子太兇猛；狐狸、猴子又太狡猾。還是讓勤勞的牛，吃苦的馬，忠心的狗，和捉老鼠的貓，去幫人類做事吧。」

但是怎麼樣才能渡過大海？才能把水稻和動物送到那邊去？牛、馬和狗都會游水，不用愁；貓不會游水，需要幫忙；水稻也需要牠們

用身子黏著稻粒帶去。玉皇大帝問水牛：「你能不能帶著稻種去？」水牛答說：「我的毛太短太細，沒法子黏緊稻粒。」玉皇大帝又問馬。馬回答說：「我因為要幫助貓，所以沒有法子兼顧。」再問狗。狗一口答應，只是牠不敢擔保，半路上不會有一些損失。

於是，牠們動身出發。牛在前面開路；馬的背上蹲著一隻小貓，在後面跟著；狗全身沾滿了金黃色的稻粒；牠們在海浪中努力向前游去。

這三個游泳的好手，掙扎到了陸地，結果狗帶來的稻穀都被沖洗淨盡，只剩下翹出水面尾巴尖兒上的一小撮；所以後來種出來的水稻，只結出一簇稻穗，都好像短短的狗尾巴似的。不過，我們人類已經覺得非常滿足。這四種動物也都成了人類的好幫手；但他們的待遇卻不一樣，牛和馬只給吃草；狗吃米飯；貓也可以吃米飯，不過那還是狗分給牠的呢。

Ⅰ. 生字與生詞

1. 狗（ㄍㄡˇ; gǒu）
   N：a dog

2. 稻子（ㄉㄠˋ·ㄗ; dàutz）
   N：unhulled rice

3. 原始時代（ㄩㄢˊ ㄕˇ ㄕˊ ㄉㄞˋ; yuánshǐshŕdài）
   N：the primeval ages
   在原始時代，人類就知道怎樣生火了。
   In the primeval ages, mankind knew how to make fire.

4. 灌木（ㄍㄨㄢˋ ㄇㄨˋ; guànmù）
   N：shrubs

5. 叢生（ㄘㄨㄥˊ ㄕㄥ; tsúngshēng）
   FV：lush and dense growth；grow thickly
   你該整理你的花園了，不要讓雜草叢生。
   You should tidy up your yard, don't let it get overgrown with weeds.

6. 毒蛇（ㄉㄨˊ ㄕㄜˊ; dúshé）
   N：venomous snake(s)

7. 猛獸（ㄇㄥˇ ㄕㄡˋ; měngshòu）
   N：fierce wild beasts

8. **艱苦**（ㄐㄧㄢ ㄎㄨˇ；jiānkǔ）
   SV：trying and hard；hardship
   你小的時候，家裡生活艱苦嗎？
   When you were young, did your family suffer hardship?

9. **玉皇大帝**（ㄩˋ ㄏㄨㄤˊ ㄉㄚˋ ㄉㄧˋ；yùhuángdàdì）
   N：the Jade Emperor；the supreme deity

10. **召開**（ㄓㄠˋ ㄎㄞ；jàukāi）
    FV：to convene or call (a meeting)
    我們公司明天要召開一個緊急會議。
    Our company will call an urgent meeting tomorrow.

11. **天神**（ㄊㄧㄢ ㄕㄣˊ；tiānshén）
    N：heavenly deities

12. **創造**（ㄔㄨㄤˋ ㄗㄠˋ；chuàngtzàu）
    FV：to create
    人類真的是上帝創造的嗎？
    Was mankind really created by God?

13. **昆蟲**（ㄎㄨㄣ ㄔㄨㄥˊ；kuēnchúng）
    N：insects

14. **蓬勃**（ㄆㄥˊ ㄅㄛˊ；péngbó）
    SV：prospering；flourishing
    當春天來臨時，大地充滿著蓬勃的生命。
    When spring comes, the Earth is covered with budding life.

15. 驚擾（ㄐㄧㄥ ㄖㄠˇ；jīngrǎu）

    FV：to disturb；to cause trouble to others；disturbed
    戰爭的消息驚擾了全國的民心。
    The news of the war disturbed the people in the whole country.

16. 恐懼（ㄎㄨㄥˇ ㄐㄩˋ；kǔngjiù）

    SV：frightened；fear；dread
    黑暗讓我恐懼。
    Darkness makes me frightened.

17. 搏鬥（ㄅㄛˊ ㄉㄡˋ；bódòu）

    FV：to fight and struggle
    人應該要和艱苦的生活搏鬥，不該輕易放棄。
    People should struggle with a hard life and not give up easily.

18. 爭奪（ㄓㄥ ㄉㄨㄛˊ；jēngduó）

    FV：to struggle over；to scramble for；to contend for
    他不想和他的兄弟爭奪他父親的財產。
    He doesn't want to fight with his brothers and sisters for his father's property.

19. 違反（ㄨㄟˊ ㄈㄢˇ；wéifǎn）

    FV：to violate（law；rules）；to contradict
    請你小心開車，不要違反交通規則，好嗎？
    Could you please drive carefully and not violate the traffic rules?

20. 屠殺（ㄊㄨˊ ㄕㄚ；túshā）
   FV：to massacre
   N：a massacre
   人類不該隨便屠殺動物。
   Mankind shouldn't casually massacre animals.

21. 慈悲（ㄘˊ ㄅㄟ；tszbēi）
   SV：kindness；mercy；clemency
   你有一副慈悲的好心腸嗎？
   Do you have a kind and merciful heart?

22. 盤古（ㄆㄢˊ ㄍㄨˇ；pángǔ）
   N：Pán Gǔ, the legendary creator and first ruler of the universe

23. 利爪（ㄌㄧˋ ㄓㄨㄚˇ；lìjuǎ）
   N：sharp claws

24. 尖牙（ㄐㄧㄢ ㄧㄚˊ；jiānyá）
   N：sharp teeth

25. 長角（ㄔㄤˊ ㄐㄧㄠˇ；chángjiǎu）
   N：long horns

26. 大翼（ㄉㄚˋ ㄧˋ；dàyì）
   N：big wings

27. 靈巧（ㄌㄧㄥˊ ㄑㄧㄠˇ；língchiǎu）

SV：clever；dexterous
她有一雙靈巧的手。
She has a pair of dexterous hands.

28. 維持（ㄨㄟˊ ㄔˊ；wéichŕ）

FV：to maintain；to sustain；to keep
他賺的薪水不夠維持全家的生活。
The salary he makes is not sufficient to maintain his whole family's living.

29. 繁衍（ㄈㄢˊ ㄧㄢˇ；fányǎn）

FV：proliferate
那一種動物繁衍得最快？
Which animal breeds the fastest?

30. 神農（ㄕㄣˊ ㄋㄨㄥˊ；shénnúng）

N：Shén Núng, the legendary ruler who introduced agriculture and herbal medicine.

31. 節育（ㄐㄧㄝˊ ㄩˋ；jiéyù）

VO：birth control；to practice birth control

32. 專靠（ㄓㄨㄢ ㄎㄠˋ；juānkàu）

FV：to specifically depend on
你是專靠養魚為生嗎？
Do you only depend on raising fish for a living?

33. 糧食（ㄌㄧㄤˊ ㄕˊ；liángshŕ）

N：foodstuff；provisions；grains

34. 獅子 (ㄕ · ㄗ ; shr̄tz)
   N：lion (s)

35. 兇猛 (ㄒㄩㄥ ㄇㄥˇ ; shiūngměng)
   SV：fierce；violent
   老虎是兇猛的動物。
   Tigers are fierce animals.

36. 狡滑 (ㄐㄧㄠˇ ㄏㄨㄚˊ ; jiǎuhuá)
   SV：cunning；sly；crafty
   聽說狐狸和狼都很狡滑。
   It is said that foxes and wolves are very cunning.

37. 勤勞 (ㄑㄧㄣˊ ㄌㄠˊ ; chínláu)
   SV：diligent；industrious；hard working
   你認爲中國人勤勞嗎？
   Do you think the Chinese are diligent and industrious?

38. 忠心 (ㄓㄨㄥ ㄒㄧㄣ ; jūngshīn)
   SV：loyal；faithful；loyalty；faithfulness
   狗對主人很忠心。
   Dogs are very loyal to their masters.

39. 渡 (ㄉㄨˋ ; dù)
   FV：to cross (a river or ocean)；to pass through (a stage, time, a check point)
   我希望早日渡過難關。
   I hope to pass through this difficult stage soon.

40. 兼顧（ㄐㄧㄢ ㄍㄨˋ；jiāngù）

FV：to take care of the needs, etc. of two things or parties
你覺得女人可以同時兼顧事業和家庭嗎？
Do you think a woman can take care of her career and family at the same time?

41. 擔保（ㄉㄢ ㄅㄠˇ；dānbǎu）

FV：to guarantee
你能擔保明天一定不會下雨嗎？
Can you guarantee it (definitely) won't rain tomorrow?

42. 損失（ㄙㄨㄣˇ ㄕ；suěnshr̄）

N：losses；casualty
這次大火造成我們很大的損失。
This big fire caused us a great loss.

43. 蹲（ㄉㄨㄣ；duēn）

FV：to squat；to crouch
我不習慣蹲太久。
I'm not used to squatting for a long time.

44. 沾（ㄓㄢ；jān）

FV：to be stuck to or marked with
冰淇淋沾到臉上了。
The ice cream was stucked on your face.

45. 掙扎（ㄓㄥ ㄓㄚˊ；jēngjá）

FV：to struggle or strive for；struggle

他一直在內心裡不停地掙扎；不能做決定。
He has been struggling within himself without cease, and can not make a decision.

46. 稻穀（ㄉㄠˋ ㄍㄨˇ；dàugǔ）
    N：rice kernel

47. 沖洗（ㄔㄨㄥ ㄒㄧˇ；chūngshǐ）
    FV：to wash with running water
    請你把車子沖洗一下。
    Could you please wash down the car a little.

48. 淨盡（ㄐㄧㄥˋ ㄐㄧㄣˋ；jingjìn）
    SV：completely exhausted (stocks, supplies, etc.)

49. 翹出（ㄑㄧㄠˋ ㄔㄨ；chiàuchū）
    RE：to stick up, out of, or across
    他把腳從桌底翹出來。
    He stuck his legs out from under the table.

50. 撮（ㄘㄨㄛˋ；tsuò）
    M：a pinch of

51. 簇（ㄘㄨˋ；tsù）
    M：a cluster

52. 稻穗（ㄉㄠˋ ㄙㄨㄟˋ；dàusuèi）
    N：the ear or spike of the rice plant
    秋天時，陽光下一簇簇金黃色的稻穗看起來很美。

In Autumn, under the sunlight the clusters of golden rice ears look very beauliful.

II. 成　語

1. 和平相處（ㄏㄜˊ ㄆㄧㄥˊ ㄒㄧㄤ ㄔㄨˇ; hépíngshiāng-chǔ）

   get along peacefully；peaceful coexistence
   如果全世界的人類都能和平相處的話，那世界上就不會有戰爭。
   If all the people in the world could get along peacefully, then the world wouldn't have wars.

III. 練　習

1. 用下列詞語造句：

    1) 時代
    2) 生活
    3) 艱苦
    4) 大地
    5) 屠殺
    6) 足夠
    7) 維持
    8) 靠
    9) 幫助
    10) 翹

2. 回答下列問題:

   1)原始時代,人類生活在什麼樣的環境裡?
   2)玉皇大帝創造萬物的原意是什麼?
   3)盤古認爲玉皇大帝給了人類什麼?
   4)人類應該滿足嗎?
   5)神農有什麼不同的看法?
   6)神農教導人類做什麼?
   7)請述説貓、狗、牛、馬四種動物的特性。
   8)狗爲人類帶來什麼東西?
   9)你最喜歡那一種動物?爲什麼?
   10)你認爲人類應該節育人口,還是增加生產稻米?

第十九課　比唱山歌

　　羅秀才是鎮上最有學問的人。他雖然很有學問，卻找不到適當工作，閒居在家，撰寫山歌。他寫好了，唸給家人聽，誰也覺得缺少趣味，因爲他寫的太正經文雅，又不自然順口，離開我們日常的生活太遠了，一般人哪裏懂啊！

　　他的妹妹勸他寫山歌，應該多抒發些男人女人的愛呀情啊的，才適合大眾的口味。他答應了，又作了許多吟唱愛情的山歌，還是一本一本地放在家裏。

　　劉三妹是一位遠近知名的才女，識字能書，插花煮茶，刺繡繪畫，縫衣烹飪，樣樣都行。唱山歌更是拿手。她和人比賽唱山歌，從來沒輸過一次。她很自負地說：

— 219 —

220 中國寓言故事

「現在，我要跟男人比唱山歌，誰要能贏了我；我就嫁給他！」

羅秀才聽到了這個消息，滿心想自己一定可以贏過她，可以娶她做老婆，就運了幾船好山歌，去見劉三妹。他到了她的屋前，碰到一個年輕的姑娘，在河邊石頭上唱歌。他向前問道：「這位姑娘，請問劉三妹的家是在這裏嗎？」

「先生貴姓？找劉三妹做什麼？」

「我是羅秀才，剛從台山來。聽說有個劉姑娘，山歌唱得聒聒叫，人也長得很漂亮。我想跟她比一比，看一看誰的山歌唱得妙？」

「你有多少山歌？敢跟她比唱！」

「我的山歌有九船：三船在福建，三船在海南，三船已撐到這河邊。」

「你還是回去吧；你不是她的對手。」

「怎麼說？」

劉三妹高聲唱道：

「石上劉三妹，

路上羅秀才，

人人山歌肚中出，

哪有山歌船撐來？」

　　唱得羅秀才一時間對答不出山歌來。他回到船上去，翻遍了船裏的山歌，還是對答不上，窘得他臉紅耳赤，將帶來的三船山歌，全扔進了河裏。

Ⅰ. 生字與生詞

1. 山歌（ㄕㄢ ㄍㄜ；shāngē）
   N：the folk songs of farmers, shepherds, woodcutters, etc

2. 羅秀才（ㄌㄨㄛˊ ㄒㄧㄡˋ ㄘㄞˊ；luóshiòutsái）
   N：Luó Shiòu-tsái, a person's name
   秀才 N：a scholar; the lowest degree conferred upon successful candidates under the civil service examination system of the Míng and Chīng Dynasties

3. 閒居（ㄒㄧㄢˊ ㄐㄩ；shiánjiū）
   FV：to lead an idle, leisurely and relaxed life
   他在退休以後，就一直閒居在家。
   Since retiring, he has led a leisurely life.

4. 撰寫（ㄓㄨㄢˋ ㄒㄧㄝˇ；juànshiě）
   FV：to write or compose
   我的爸爸正在撰寫一本小說。
   My father is presently writing a novel.

5. 缺少（ㄑㄩㄝ ㄕㄠˇ；chiuēshǎu）
   FV：lacking; deficient
   你有沒有覺得你的生活中缺少些什麼呢？
   Do you feel your life is lacking something?

6. 趣味（ㄑㄩˋ ㄨㄟˋ；chiùwèi）
   N：to be interesting

這本書一點趣味也沒有。
This book is of absolutely no interest.

7. 正經 (ㄓㄥˋ ㄐㄧㄥ ; jèngyīng)

SV：very proper ; serious ; decent ; respectable
他這個人看起來很正經。
He looks very decent.

8. 一般 (ㄧˋ ㄅㄢ ; yìbān)

SV：common ; general
一般說來，他待我很好。
Generally speaking, he is kind to me.

9. 抒發 (ㄕㄨ ㄈㄚ ; shūfā)

FV：to express ; to give expression to
唱歌可以抒發我們的心情。
Singing can express our moods.

10. 口味 (ㄎㄡˇ ㄨㄟˋ ; kǒuwèi)

N：taste
我們的口味很接近。
Our tastes are very close.

11. 劉三妹 (ㄌㄧㄡˊ ㄙㄢ ㄇㄟˋ ; lióusānmèi)

N：Lióu Sān-mèi, woman's name

12. 插花 (ㄔㄚ ㄏㄨㄚ ; chāhuā)

VO：to arrange flowers ; flower arrangement

13. 煮茶（ㄓㄨˇ ㄔㄚˊ；jǔchá）
    VO：to boil tea

14. 刺繡（ㄘˋ ㄒㄧㄡˋ；tsžshiòu）
    FV：to embroider
    N：embroidery

15. 縫衣（ㄈㄥˊ ㄧ；féngyī）
    VO：to sew；sewing

16. 烹飪（ㄆㄥ ㄖㄣˋ；pēngrèn）
    FV：to cook；cooking

17. 拿手（ㄋㄚˊ ㄕㄡˇ；náshǒu）
    SV & AT：one's special skill or ability；to be particularly good or dexterous at
    英文是我最拿手的科目。
    English is my best subject.

18. 比賽（ㄅㄧˇ ㄙㄞˋ；bǐsài）
    N：a contest；a match；a tournament
    FV：to compete in a contest, etc.
    我們來比賽，看誰跑得快。
    Let's have a race to see who can run faster.

19. 輸（ㄕㄨ；shū）
    FV：to lose
    他昨天打麻將，輸了兩千元。

He played mah-jong yesterday and lost two thousand dollars.

20. 自負（ㄗˋ ㄈㄨˋ；tzfù）

AT：to have a high opinion of oneself；conceited
他是個很自負的人。
He is quite a conceited person.

21. 贏（ㄧㄥˊ；yíng）

FV：to win
在比賽中每個人都喜歡贏
Everybody likes to win in a contest.

22. 運（ㄩㄣˋ；yùn）

FV：to transport；to move
這些東西都是從香港運來的。
These things were all transported from Hong Kong.

23. 姑娘（ㄍㄨ・ㄋㄧㄤ；gū-niang）

N：an unmarried girl

24. 台山（ㄊㄞˊ ㄕㄢ；táishān）

N：an area in Guǎng-dūng Province（廣東省）

25. 聒聒叫（ㄍㄨㄚ ㄍㄨㄚ ㄐㄧㄠˋ；guāguājiàu）

IE：very good；wonderful；excellent
我弟弟游泳游得聒聒叫。
My younger brother swims really well.

26. 福建（ㄈㄨˊ ㄐㄧㄢˋ；fújiàn）

   N：Fú-jiàn Province

27. 海南（ㄏㄞˇ ㄋㄢˊ；hǎinán）

   N：Hǎi-nán Province

28. 撐（ㄔㄥ；chēng）

   FV：to pole (a boat)；to punt
   他把船撐到河邊。
   He poled the boat to hte bank of the river.

29. 對手（ㄉㄨㄟˋ ㄕㄡˇ；duèishǒu）

   N：an opponent
   說到游泳，你不是他的對手。
   As for swimming, you are no match for him.

30. 對答（ㄉㄨㄟˋ ㄉㄚˊ；duèidá）

   FV：to give an answer；to reply
   她的話讓我一時對答不出來。
   Her words made me momentarily unable to reply.

31. 翻遍（ㄈㄢ ㄅㄧㄢˋ；fānbiàn）

   RE：to turn through all (the pages of a book, etc.)
   我整本字典都翻遍了，就是找不到這個字。
   I have leafed through my dictionary, but I just can't find this word.

II. 成語

1. **遠近知名** (ㄩㄢˇ ㄐㄧㄣˋ ㄓ ㄇㄧㄥˊ；yuǎnjìnjrmíng)

    be known far and near
    我妹妹從小就是個遠近知名的美女。
    Ever since she was young, my sister has been known as a beauty near and far.

2. **樣樣都行** (ㄧㄤˋ ㄧㄤˋ ㄉㄡ ㄒㄧㄥˊ；yàngyàngdōushíng)

    accomplished in everything ; master of all trader
    他是個有才能的人，什麼都會，樣樣都行。
    He is a talented person who knows everything, and is accomplished in everything.

3. **臉紅耳赤** (ㄌㄧㄢˇ ㄏㄨㄥˊ ㄦˇ ㄔˋ；liǎnhúngěrchr̀)

    (Lit) Face and ears turn red (blush with shame)
    我一生氣就臉紅耳赤。
    As soon as I'm angry, I go all red.

III. 詞組與句型

1. **自從⋯，從來沒**

    Ever since..., have never
    自從我結婚以來，從來沒有煮過飯。
    Ever since I got married, I haven't made a meal.
    自從他從美國回來後，從來沒去「麥當勞」吃過東西。
    Ever since he came back from the States, he hasn't eaten anything at MacDonalds.

IV. 練　習

1. 用下列詞語造句：

　　1)學問
　　2)工作
　　3)趣味
　　4)大眾
　　5)吟唱
　　6)姑娘
　　7)對手
　　8)對答
　　9)窘得
　　10)扔進

2. 回答下列問題：

　　1)羅秀才為什麼撰寫山歌？
　　2)羅秀才的妹妹認為山歌應當寫些什麼樣的內容？
　　3)羅秀才有沒有作出好聽好唱的山歌呢？
　　4)劉三妹是如何的一位才女？
　　5)比唱山歌，是怎麼樣的一種比賽法？
　　6)羅秀才運了多少船的山歌，去參加比賽？
　　7)在河邊石頭上唱歌的年輕姑娘，是誰？
　　8)為什麼說：「山歌肚中出」？
　　9)為什麼又說：「哪有山歌船撐來？」
　　10)你如果是羅秀才，你將怎麼樣回唱？

第二十課　梅花的故事

　　過去，中國人對婚姻的看法，很注重門當戶對，不相配的婚姻就說是癩蝦蟆想吃天鵝肉，一朵鮮花插在牛糞上。沒錢的青年，要想娶富家女兒，那是比上天還難。

　　現在我要說的是梅花與愛情有關的故事。

　　有一個老農夫很有錢；他有一個女兒長得很漂亮，所以有許多青年來求婚！像賣珠寶的小吳，送她一個大鑽戒；她看都不看一眼。賣綢緞的劉老闆，送她最漂亮的衣服；她也不要。開飯店的王先生，說可以讓她天天吃好吃的東西；她也不喜歡。她偏偏愛上了在他父親農場工作的牛仔黃。老農夫氣得鬍子都翹起來了。最後決定把牛仔黃趕了出去，說：「小伙子，滾出去，我永遠不要再見到你！」

中國寓言故事

牛仔黃非常傷心地走了。她追著去送他，一直追到十里長亭才追上！他們在階前坐了下來，天也黑了，沒有月亮，天空佈滿濃濃的雲。她說：「我們在這樣的荒野裡？你怕不怕？」

「不怕，我只怕我們分離。」牛仔黃說。

「不要想這些。祖母最疼我了，明天一早，我們就去祖母家，求她向父親說說情。」

空中的雲越來越密，天氣越來越冷，開始飄起一片片美麗的雪花。他們悲傷的眼淚，一顆顆凝結成珠子，掉落在雪地上。下了一夜的大雪，不到半夜就淹沒了他們兩個人。他們凍僵了的手臂互相擁抱著。

第二天，他們成了兩棵梅樹，一棵開著紅艷的花，一棵開著雪白的花。過路的人說：紅花是這個農家女變的，白花是那個牛仔黃變的，所以以後每到雪花紛飛的寒冬，他們就會開起花來，表現他們堅貞不渝的愛情，傲然超俗的精神。

I. 生字與生詞

1. 梅花（ㄇㄟˊ ㄏㄨㄚ；méihuā）
   N：plum blossoms

2. 婚姻（ㄏㄨㄣ ㄧㄣ；huēnyīn）
   N：marriage
   祝你們有個美滿的婚姻。
   Wishing you a happy marriage.

3. 注重（ㄓㄨˋ ㄓㄨㄥˋ；jùjùng）
   FV：to emphasize；to attach importance to
   西方人很注重餐桌上的禮儀。
   Westerners place importance on table etiquette.

4. 相配（ㄒㄧㄤ ㄆㄟˋ；shiāngpèi）
   FV：to match each other
   你的衣服和鞋子不相配。
   Your clothes and shoes don't match.

5. 吳（ㄨˊ；wú）
   N：Wu, a surname

6. 鑽戒（ㄗㄨㄢˋ ㄐㄧㄝˋ；tzuànjiè）
   N：a diamond ring
   鑽石（ㄗㄨㄢˋ ㄕˊ；tzuànshŕ）
   diamond(s)
   戒子（ㄐㄧㄝˋ・ㄗ；jietz）

a ring

7. 綢緞（ㄔㄡˊ ㄉㄨㄢˋ；chóuduàn）
    N：silk goods

8. 牛仔黃（ㄋㄧㄡˊ ㄗㄞˇ ㄏㄨㄤˊ；nióutzǎihuáng）
    N：Cowboy Huáng (a name)

9. 鬍子（ㄏㄨˊ・ㄗ；hútz）
    N：a beard

10. 小伙子（ㄒㄧㄠˇ ㄏㄨㄛˇ・ㄗ；shiǎuhuǒtz）
    N：young guy
    你是個很高大的小伙子。
    You are a very tall young guy.

11. 滾出去（ㄍㄨㄣˇ ㄔㄨ ㄑㄩˋ；guěnchūchiù）
    DC：get lost；get out of here
    你馬上給我滾出去。
    Get out of my sight, right now!
    滾　FV：to roll

12. 十里長亭（ㄕˊ ㄌㄧˇ ㄔㄤˊ ㄊㄧㄥˊ；shrlǐchángtíng）
    N：small pavilions every 10 lǐ for travelers to rest

13. 階（ㄐㄧㄝ；jiē）
    N：steps；stairs

14. 佈（ㄅㄨˋ；bù）

FV：to cover；to arrange
天空佈滿了黑雲，好像要下雨了。
The sky is completely covered with clouds. It looks like it'll rain.

15. 荒野（ㄏㄨㄤ ㄧㄝˇ；huāngyě）

N：the wilderness
聽說從前有個小孩在荒野裡和狼群一起長大。
I heard there once was a child who grew up with a pack of wolves in the wilderness.

16. 祖母（ㄗㄨˇ ㄇㄨˇ；tzǔmǔ）

N：grandmother (father's mother)

17. 疼（ㄊㄥˊ；téng）

FV：to be fond (of a child)
我的媽媽很疼我。
My mother is very fond of me.

18. 密（ㄇㄧˋ；mì）

SV：dense；intimate
台灣的人口很密。
Taiwan has a high population density.

19. 悲傷（ㄅㄟ ㄕㄤ；bēishāng）

SV：sad；sorrowful；sadness
請你不要悲傷。
Please don't be sad.

20. 凝結（ㄋㄧㄥˊ ㄐㄧㄝˊ；níngjié）

   FV：to condense（gas to liquid）；to solidify or congeal（liquid to solid）
   在很冷的地方，人的鼻水有時會凝結成冰。
   In cold places, sometimes people's nasal drippings solidify into ice.

21. 淹沒（ㄧㄢ ㄇㄛˋ；yānmò）

   FV：submerged；inundated
   我家院子的花草被昨晚的大雨淹沒了。
   The plants in my yard were submerged in last night's heavy rain.

22. 凍僵（ㄉㄨㄥˋ ㄐㄧㄤ；dùngjiāng）

   RC：to be frozen stiff
   天氣太冷了，我的鼻子都快凍僵了。
   It's got really cold, my nose is almost frozen solid.

23. 手臂（ㄕㄡˇ ㄅㄟˋ；shǒubèi）

   N：the arm from the wrist up

24. 成（ㄔㄥˊ；chéng）

   FV：to transform into；to become
   我們應該把悲傷化成力量。
   We should transform sadness into power.

25. 紅艷（ㄏㄨㄥˊ ㄧㄢˋ；húngyàn）

   SV：rich red

院子裡的玫瑰很紅豔。
The roses in the yard are of rich red color.

26. 雪花（ㄒㄩㄝˇ ㄏㄨㄚ ; shiuěhuā）

N：snowflakes

27. 紛飛（ㄈㄣ ㄈㄟ ; fēnfēi）

FV：to fly all over ; to whirl around in confusion
你看過雪花紛飛的早晨嗎？
Have you seen a morning of whirling snow flakes?

28. 寒冬（ㄏㄢˊ ㄉㄨㄥ ; hándūng）

N：a cold winter
當寒冬來臨時，我總是很難從床上爬起來。
When the cold winter comes, it's always difficult for me to get out of bed.

II. 成　語

1. 門當戶對（ㄇㄣˊ ㄉㄤ ㄏㄨˋ ㄉㄨㄟˋ ; méndānghùduèi）

(Lit) The doors of both sides are well matched. (Marry with one's match.)
families of equal standing (usually referring to those of a married couple) ; well matched
他爸爸是醫生，而她的爸爸是律師，他們要結婚，真可以說是門當戶對。
His father is a doctor, her father is a lawyer, and they want to get married. You could say their families are of equal

standing.

2. 癩蝦蟆想吃天鵝肉（ㄌㄞˋ ㄏㄚˊ ˙ㄇㄚ ㄒㄧㄤˇ ㄔ ㄊㄧㄢ ㄜˊ ㄖㄡˋ；làihámǎ shiǎngchrtiān-érou）

The ugly toad wants to eat swan meat (lit.) refers to a male suitor who doesn't have the qualifications, or attributes to ask a woman for her hand in marriage.

3. 一朵鮮花插在牛糞上（ㄧˋ ㄉㄨㄛˇ ㄒㄧㄢ ㄏㄨㄚ ㄔㄚ ㄗㄞˋ ㄋㄧㄡˊ ㄈㄣˋ ㄕㄤˋ；yiduǒshiānhuā chātzàinióufènshàng）

A fresh flower is stuck in cow stool (lit.), refers to an unequal marriage where the wife is much younger, better looking, or smarter than the husband.

4. 堅貞不渝（ㄐㄧㄢ ㄓㄣ ㄅㄨˋ ㄩˊ；jiānjēnbùyú）

unyielding
(unchanging) faithfulness
他們堅貞不渝的愛情很感人。
Their unchanging faithfulness in love is very touching.

5. 傲然超俗（ㄠˋ ㄖㄢˊ ㄔㄠ ㄙㄨˊ；aùránchāusú）

Haughty bone and free from vulgarity.
uncommonly proud hearted and afraid of nothing
梅花有一種傲然超俗的氣質。
Plum blossoms have a proud and courageous disposition.

III. 詞組與句型

1. 對⋯看法　concerning⋯opinion

你對婚姻有什麼看法？
What do you think of marriage?
你對他這個人的看法怎麼樣。
What is your opinion of him?

2. 與⋯有關　connetion with⋯concern；to be related to⋯

你的工作與那一方面有關？
What is your job concerned with?
我今天要告訴你一件與你有關的消息。
Today I want to tell you some news concerning you.

IV. 練　習

1. 用下列詞語造句：

　　1) 婚姻
　　2) 相配
　　3) 就說
　　4) 有關
　　5) 長得
　　6) 也不要
　　7) 非常
　　8) 佈滿
　　9) 最

10)成

2. 回答下列問題：

　　1)中國人常用什麼情況來比喻不相配的婚姻？
　　2)癩蛤蟆和天鵝為什麼不相配？
　　3)鮮花和牛糞為什麼不相配？
　　4)鑽戒、綢緞，農家女看都不看一眼，那她要什麼？
　　5)老農夫為什麼反對牛仔黃追求他的女兒？
　　6)農家女和牛仔黃的愛情，結局如何？
　　7)十里長亭的兩棵梅樹是怎麼來的？
　　8)紅色的梅花有什麼象徵的含意？
　　9)白色的梅花有什麼象徵的含意？
　10)老農夫「門當戶對」的觀念，錯了嗎？

附錄一　詞類略語表

A	Adverb
AT	Attributive
AV	Auxiliary Verb
B	Unclassified Bound Form
CV	Coverb
DC	Directional Complement
DV	Directional Verb
FV	Functive Verb
I	Interjection
IE	Idiomatic Expression
L	Localizer
M	Measure
N	Noun
NU	Number
ON	Onomatopoetic Term
P	Particle
PN	Pronoun
PT	Pattern
PV	Post Verb
PW	Place Word
QW	Question Word
RC	Resultative Compound
RE	Resultative Ending
SP	Specifier
SV	Stative Verb
TW	Time Word
VO	Verb Object Compound

附錄二　世界中文報業協會三千個基本常用字彙表中的一千個最常用字

A

		bǎu	寶	biǎu	表(錶)
A		bàu	抱	bié	別
à,ā,e	阿	bàu	報		
ài	愛	bèi,bēi	背	**C**	
ān	安	běi	北	chá	茶
àn	暗	bèi	備	chá	察
àn	案	bèi	被	chǎn	產
		běn	本	chāng	昌
		bǐ,bì	比	cháng,jǎng	長
B		bǐ	筆	cháng,chǎng	場
bā,	八	bì	必	cháng	常
bǎ,bà	把	bì	畢	chǎng	廠
bà	爸	bìng	並	chàng	唱
bà,ba	罷	bìng	并	cháu,jāu	朝
ba	吧	bìng	病	chē,jiū	車
bái,bó	白	bǔ	補	chě	扯
bǎi,bó	百	bù	不	chén,shén	沉(沈)
bài	敗	bù	布	chén	晨
bān	般	bù	佈	chén	陳
bān	頒	bù	步	chēng,chèng	稱
bǎn	板	bù	部	chéng	成
bǎn	版	bù	簿	chéng	城
bàn	半	bó,bǎi	伯	chéng	程
bàn	辦	biān	編	chéng,shèng	乘
bàng	棒	biān	邊	chī	七
bāu	包	biàn	變	chī,chí	期
bāu	胞	biǎu	標	chí	奇
bǎ	保				

chí	其		創(剏)	dà,dài	大
chí	旗	chuēi	吹	dài	代
chí	齊	chuēn	春	dài	待
chǐ	起	chiān	千	dài	帶
chǐ	啟(啓)	chián	前	dān,dàn	擔(担)
chì	汽	chián	錢	dān,shàn	單
chì	氣	chiāng	槍(鎗)	dàn	但
chì	器	chiáng	牆	dàn	淡(澹)
chīn	侵	chiǎng,chiǎng, jiàng		dàn,tán	彈
chīn	親		強	dāng,dàng	當
chīng	青	chiáu	僑	dǎng	黨
chīng	清	chiáu	橋	dāu	刀
chīng,chíng	傾	chiē,chiè	切	dǎu	島
chīng	輕	chiě	且	dǎu,dàu	倒
chíng	情	chiōu	秋	dàu	道
chǐng	請	chióu	求	dàu	到
chìng	慶	chióu	球	dàu,dǎu	導
chr̄	吃(喫)	chiū	區	dàu	稻
chř,chě	尺	chiǔ	取	dé,děi,de	得
chū	出	chiù	去	dēng	燈
chū	初	chiún	羣(群)	děng	等
chú	除	chiuán	全	dī	低
chǔ,chù	處	chiuán	權	dí	敵
chūng	充	chiuè	卻(却)	dǐ	底
chúng,jùng	重	chiuè	確	dǐ	抵
chúng	蟲			dì,de,dí	的
chuān	穿			dì	地
chuán	船	dā,dá	答	dì	弟
chuāng	窗	dá	達	dì	第
chuāng,chuàng		dǎ,dá	打	dì	定
				dìng	

D

dìng	訂	fá,fǎ,fà	法		**G**	
dōu,dū	都	fǎn	反			
dú	獨	fǎn	返	gāi		該
dú	毒	fàn	飯	gǎi		改
dú,dòu	讀	fàn	範	gài		概
dù	度	fāng	方	gān		甘
dūng	冬	fáng	房	gǎn		敢
dūng	東	fǎng	訪	gǎn		感
dùng	動	fàng	放	gàn		幹(榦)
duān	端	fēi	非	gāng		剛
duǎn	短	féi	肥	gāng		鋼
duàn	段	fěi	匪	gǎng		港
duàn	斷	fèi	費	gāu		高
duèi	隊	fèi	廢	gàu		告
duèi	對	fēn,fèn	分	gē		哥
duō	多	fěn	粉	gē		歌
diǎn	典	fèn	份	gé		革
diǎn	點	fēng	風	gé		格
diàn	店	fēng	豐	gè		各
diàn	電	fū	夫	gè,ge		個(箇)
diàu,tiáu	調	fú	服	gěi,jǐ		給
		fú	福	gēn		根
	E		fǔ	府	gēn		跟
é,è	俄	fù	父	gèng,gēng,jīng		更
ér	而	fù	附	gòu		夠(够)
ér	兒	fù	赴	gòu		構
ěr	耳	fù	負	gǔ		古
		fù	副	gù		故
	F		fù	富	gūng		工
fā	發	fù	復	gūng		公

gūng	功	háng	航	huéi	回		
gūng	攻	hǎu,hàu	好	huèi,kwài	會		
gūng,gùng	供	hàu,háu	號	huó	活		
gùng	共	hé	合	huǒ	火		
guài	怪	hé,hàn,huo,hè	和	huò	或		
guān	官	hé	河	huò	貨		
guān,guàn	觀	hé	何				
guān	關(関)	hēi	黑	**J**			
guǎn	管	hěn	很	jǎn	展		
guǎn	館(舘)	hòu	候	jàn	占(佔)		
guàn	慣	hòu	後	jàn	站		
guāng	光	hū	呼	jàn	戰		
guǎng	廣	hū	忽	jāng	章		
guēi	規	hù	戶	jāng	張		
guēi	歸	hù	護	jāu	招		
guèi	貴	húng	紅	jāu,jáu,je,jù,juó			
guó	國	huā	花		著(着)		
guǒ	果	huá	華	jàu,shàu	召		
guò	過	huà,huá	劃	jàu	照		
		huà	化	jě	者		
H		huà	話	je,jèi	這		
hái	孩	huà	畫	jēn	針		
hái,huán	還	huái	懷	jēn	真		
hǎi	海	huài	壞	jèn	陣		
hài	害	huān	歡(懽)	jèn	振		
hán	含	huán	環	jèn	鎮		
hán	寒	huàn	喚	jēng	爭		
hán	韓	huàn	換	jěng	整		
hǎn	喊	huáng	皇	jèng,jēng	正		
hàn	漢	huáng	黃	jèng	政		

附錄二 249

jēng	證(証)	jīng	驚	jū	諸	
jī	基	jǐng,yǐng	景	jú	竹	
jī	積	jǐng	警	jú	築	
jī	機	jìng	竟	jǔ	主	
jí	及	jìng	淨	jù	住	
jí	吉	jìng	境	jù	注	
jí	集	jìng	敬	jù	助	
jí	急	jōu	州	jūng,jùng	中	
jí	級	jōu	周	jūng	忠	
jí	即	jōu	洲	jūng	終	
jí	極	jōu	週	jùng,jǔng	種	
jí	擊	jr̄	之	jùng	眾	
jǐ	己	jr̄	支	juān	專	
jǐ,jī	幾	jr̄	枝	juǎn,juàn	轉	
jì,jǐ	季	jr̄	知	juàn,chuán	傳	
jì	濟	jr̄	隻	juāng	裝	
jì	計	jr̄	織	juàng	狀	
jì	記	jŕ	直	juēi	追	
jì	紀	jŕ	植	juěn	準	
jì	際	jŕ	質	jiā	加	
jì	繼	jŕ	職	jiā	家	
jīn	今	jř	只	jiǎ	甲	
jīn	金	jř	止	jiǎ,jià	假	
jǐn	緊	jř	紙	jià	價	
jìn	近	jr̀	至	jiān,jiàn	間	
jìn	進	jr̀	志	jiān	兼	
jìn	盡	jr̀	治	jiān	堅	
jīng	京	jr̀	制	jiǎn	減	
jīng	經	jr̀	致	jiǎn	簡	
jīng	精	jr̀	製	jiǎn	檢	

jiàn	見	jiú	局			**L**	
jiàn	件	jiǔ	舉(舉)				
jiàn	建	jiù	句	lái	來		
jiàn	健	jiù	具	láu,làu	勞		
jiàn	漸	jiù	據(据)	lǎu	老		
jiāng,jiàng	將	jiūn	均	lè,yàu,yuè	樂		
jiǎng	講	jiūn	軍	le,liǎu	了		
jiǎng	獎	jiué	決(决)	lèi	類		
jiāu	交	jiué	絕	lěng	冷		
jiāu,jiàu	教			lí	離		
jiǎu,jiué	角		**K**	lǐ	李		
jiǎu	腳(脚)	kāi	開	lǐ	里		
jiǎu,jiàu	較	kàn,kān	看	lǐ	理		
jiàu	叫	kāng	康	lǐ	裏(裡)		
jiàu,jiué	覺	kàng	抗	lǐ	禮		
jiē	接	kǎu	考(玫)	lì	力		
jiē	街	kē	科	lì	立		
jié,jiē	結	kě,kè	可	lì	利		
jié	節	kè	克	lì	例		
jié	潔	kè	客	lì	歷		
jiě	姊(姐)	kè,kē	刻	lín	林		
jiè	界	kè	課	lín	鄰(隣)		
jiōu,jiòu	究	kěn	肯	líng	零		
jiǒu	九	kǒu	口	lǐng	領		
jiǒu	久	kǔ	苦	lìng	令		
jiǒu	酒	kūng,kùng	空	lìng	另		
jiòu	救	kǔng	恐	lóu	樓		
jiòu	就	kuài	快	lù,liòu	陸		
jiòu	舊	kuài	塊	lù	路		
jiū	居	kuǎn	款	luàn	亂		

附　錄　二　251

luò,là,làu,lè	落	màn	慢	nán	男		
luén	輪	máng	忙	nán,nàn	難		
luèn	論	máu	毛	nǎu	腦		
lián	連	méi,mò	沒	ne,ní	呢		
lián	聯	měi	每	nèi	內		
liàn	練	měi	美	néng	能		
jiǎng,liàng	量	mèi	妹	ní,nī	泥		
liáng	良	mén	門	nǐ	你		
liǎng	兩	men	們	nǔ	努		
liàng	亮	mì,bì	秘	nián	年		
liàu	料	mì	密	niàn	念		
liè	列	mǐ	米	niǎu	鳥		
liè	烈	mín	民	nióu	牛		
lióu	流	míng	名	niǔ	女		
lióu	留	míng	明				
lióu	劉	mìng	命	**O**			
lióu,lù	六	mǔ	母	ōu	歐		
liǔ	旅	mù	木				
liù	律	mù	目	**P**			
liù	綠	mó	模(糢)	pà	怕		
liuè	略	mián	棉	pāi	拍		
		miǎn	免	pái	排		
M		miàn	面	pài	派		
mā	媽	miè	滅	páng	旁		
mǎ	馬			pǎu	跑		
ma	嗎	**N**		pàu	炮(砲)(礮)		
ma,me	麼	ná	拿	pèi	配		
mǎi	買	nǎ,nà,něi,nèi	那	péng	朋		
mài	賣	nǎi	乃	pí	皮		
mǎn	滿	nán	南	pin	品		

píng	平	sān,shēn,tsān	參	shòu	受	
pǔ	普	sǎn,sàn	散	shr̄	失	
pō,pǒ	頗	sǎu,sàu	掃	shr̄	施	
pō,bō	波	sè,shǎi	色	shr̄	師	
pò	破	shā	沙	shŕ	十	
piàn,biàn	便	shā	殺	shŕ,dàn	石	
piàn	片	shān	山	shŕ	拾	
piàu	票	shàn	善	shŕ	食	
		shāng	商	shŕ	時	
		shāng	傷	shŕ	實	
R		shàng,shǎng	上	shř	史	
r̀	日	shāu	燒	shř,shr̀	使	
rán	然	shǎu,shàu	少	shř	始	
rán	燃	shè	社	shr̀	士	
ràng	讓	shè	設	shr̀	世	
rè	熱	shé,shén,shèn	甚	shr̀	市	
rén	人	shéi,shuéi	誰	shr̀	式	
rén	仁	shēn	身	shr̀	是	
rèn,rén	任	shēn	深	shr̀	事	
rèn	認	shén	神	shr̀	室	
réng	仍	shēng	生	shr̀	試	
ròu	肉	shēng	升(陞)	shr̀	示	
rú	如	shēng	聲	shr̀	視	
rù	入	shěng,shǐng	省	shr̀	適	
rúng	容	shèng,chéng	盛	shr̀	勢	
rúng	榮	shèng,shēng	勝	shr̀	識	
ruò	若	shōu	收	shū	書	
		shǒu	手	shú,shóu	熟	
S		shǒu	守	shù	述	
sài	賽	shǒu	首	shù	術	
sān,sàn	三					

附錄二 253

shù	樹	shiàng	象	shíng,háng	行
shù,shǔ	數	shiàng	項	shíng	形
shuāng	雙(双)	shiàng	像	shìng	性
shuěi	水	shiāu	消	shīng	幸
shuèi	睡	shiǎu	小	shìng	姓
shuō,shuèi	說	shiàu	笑	shiōu	休
shuèn	順	shiàu,jiàu	校	shiōu	修
sù	訴	shiàu	效(効)	shiū	須
sùng	送	shiē	些	shiū	需
suàn	算	shié	協	shiǔ	許
suēi,suéi	雖	shiě	寫	shiù	續
suèi	歲	shiè	謝	shiùn	訊
suǒ	所	shī	西	shiùn	訓
suēn	孫	shī	吸	shiūng	兄
shià	下	shī	希	shiúng	雄
shià	夏	shī	悉	shiuān	宣
shiān	先	shí	息	shiuǎn	選
shiǎn	險	shí	習	shiué	學
shiàn	現	shǐ	洗	sz	司
shiàn	限	shǐ	喜	sz	私
shiàn	線(綫)	shì	系	sz	思
shiàn	縣	shì	細	sz	絲
shiàn	憲	shì	係	sž	死
shiāng,shiàng	相	shì	戲(戲)	sz̀	四
shiāng	鄉	shīn	心	sz	似
shiāng	香	shīn	辛		
shiáng	詳	shīn	新	**T**	
shiǎng	想	shìn	信	tā	他
shiǎng	響	shīng	星	tā	她
shiàng	向	shīng,shìng	興	tái	臺(台)

tài	太	tsž		tzēng,tséng		曾
tài	泰	tsz̀		tzēng		增
tài	態	tú		tzèng		贈
tán	談	tǔ		tzǒu		走
táng	糖	tǔ		tzú		足
táu	逃	tūng		tzú		族
tǎu	討	túng		tzǔ		祖
tè	特	túng		tzǔ		組
tí	提	tǔng		tzūng		宗
tí	題	tùng		tzǔng		總
tǐ	體(体)	tuán		tzuěi		嘴
tì	替	tuēi		tzuèi		罪
tīng,tìng	聽	tuèi		tzuèi		最
tíng	庭	tuō		tzuó		昨
tíng	停	tiān		tzuǒ		左
tóu	投	tián		tzuò		坐
tóu	頭	tiáu		tzuò		作
tsái	才(纔)	tiàu		tzuò		做
tsái	材	tiě				
tsái	財	tz			W	
tsǎi	採	tž		wài		外
tsài	菜	tz̀		wān		灣
tsān	餐	tz̀		wán		完
tsāu	操	tzài		wǎn		晚
tsǎu	草	tzài		wàn		萬
tsúng,tzùng	從	tzǎu		wáng		王
tsuūn	村(邨)	tzàu		wǎng,wàng		往
tsuò	錯	tzé		wàng		望
tsz	詞	tzé		wēi		威
tsz	慈	tzě,tzěn		wēi		危

附錄二 255

wéi,wèi	爲	yān	(煙)(菸)	yì		易
wéi	維	yán	言	yì		意
wéi	圍	yán	沿	yì		義
wěi,wēi	微	yán,yàn	研	yì		液
wěi,wēi	委	yán	嚴	yì		益
wěi	偉	yǎn	演	yì		議
wèi	未	yǎn	眼	yīn		因
wèi	位	yàn	驗	yīn		音
wèi	味	yāng	央	yín		銀
wèi	謂	yáng	洋	yǐn,yìn		飲
wèi	衛	yáng	陽	yìn		印
wēn	溫	yǎng	養	yīng		英
wén	文	yàng	樣	yīng,yìng		應
wén,wèn	聞	yāu	搖	yíng		迎
wèn	問	yāu,yáu	要	yǐng		影
wǒ	我	yàu	藥(药)	yìng		優
wū	屋	yě	也	yōu		由
wú	無	yè	夜	yóu		油
wǔ	午	yè	葉	yóu		遊
wǔ	五	yè	業	yǒu		友
wǔ	武	yī	一	yǒu		有
wǔ	舞	yī	衣	yòu		又
wù	物	yī	依	yòu		右
wù	誤	yī	醫	yú		于
wù	務	yí	宜	yú		於
		yí	移	yú		魚
		yí	遺	yú		餘
Y		yǐ	已	yǔ		雨
yá	牙	yǐ	以	yǔ		語
yǎ,yà	亞	yǐ	亦			
ya	呀	yì		yǔ		

yǔ,yú,yù	與
yù	玉
yù	育
yù	域
yù	遇
yù	預
yún	雲
yùn	運
yǔng	永
yǔng	勇
yùng	用
yuán	元
yuán	原
yuán	源
yuán	員
yuán	園
yuán	圓
yuǎn	遠
yuàn	院
yuàn	願
yuē	約
yuè	月
yuè	越

共：962字　　包括（一、二、三、四、五、六、七、八、九、十、拾、百、千、萬）

附錄三　本冊所用生字表
（阿拉伯數字代表課數）

	A		bó	脖	10
			bó	駁	14
àn	案	8	bó	勃	18
áng	昂	16	bó	博	18
ào	傲	20			
				C	
	B		chā	插	15
bā	巴	10	chá	查	13
bǎi	擺	5	cháng	嘗	5
bāng	傍	17	cháng	腸	14
bǎng	綁	7	chāu	超	20
bǎng	膀	7	chèn	趁	11
bǎu	飽	14	chēng	撐	19
bēi	悲	15	chéng	澄	4
bèi	臂	20	chǐ	豈	14
bēn	奔	16	chì	企	11
bēng	崩	17	chià	恰	10
bèng	蹦	6	chiān	牽	12
bì	避	6	chiǎn	淺	8
bì	陛	9	chiàu	翹	18
biàn	辯	10	chiè	竊	12
biàn	遍	11	chín	琴	16
biē	憋	13	chín	勤	18
bó	博	3	chīng	傾	16
bó	渤	8	chiúng	窮	12
bó,báu	薄	8	chóu	酬	3
bó,bǎi	柏	10	chóu	綢	20

chī	癡	2
chù	觸	9
chù	畜	13
chuǎng	闖	12
chūng	沖	18
chǔng	寵	9

D

dā	搭	2
dàn	誕	15
dǎng	擋	17
dèng	瞪	2
dī	滴	16
diàn	殿	9
diàn	奠	16
diāu	雕	3
diē	爹	7
dié	碟	5
dié	蝶	15
dǐng	頂	1
dǒu	蚪	8
dòu	豆	8
dù	妒	9
dù	渡	18
duān	端	5
duàn	緞	20
duēi	堆	9
duēn	蹲	18
dùng	凍	20
duó	奪	18

E

é	鵝	10
ēn	恩	10

F

fá	罰	12
fān	翻	13
fēn	紛	20
fén	焚	16
fèn	糞	20
féng	縫	19
fú	浮	17
fǔ	甫	14
fù	腹	14

G

gài	蓋	9
gān	杆	8
gǎn	桿	9
gāu	高	6
gē	擱	7
gēng	耕	12
gǒu	狗	18
gòu	購	3
gū	姑	19
gǔ	股	7
gǔ	鼓	16
gǔ	穀	18
gù	固	1

gù	僱	3	huǒ	伙	20
gù	顧	18	huò	獲	12
guā	颳	17			
guā	聒	19	**J**		
guà	掛	16	já	紮	13
guàn	灌	5	já	扎	18
guēi	龜	8	jān	沾	18
guěn	滾	20	jǎn	盞	10
gūng	宮	9	jǎng	掌	11
guō	郭	14	jāu	朝	14
			jē	遮	9
H			jé	轍	17
há	蝦	10	jēn	珍	3
háng	杭	14	jēn	貞	20
háu	毫	8	jěn	枕	6
hé	何	8	jēng	掙	18
hè	鶴	10	jī	激	3
hóu	猴	6	jī	稽	7
hú	湖	14	jī	譏	8
hú	蝴	15	jì	技	3
hú	鬍	20	jì	寄	16
hù	互	9	jì	祭	16
huá	滑	14	jiān	肩	7
huáng	簧	3	jiān	艱	18
huēi	灰	9	jiān	尖	18
huèi	慧	6	jiàn	鑑	16
huèi	惠	15	jiāng	僵	20
huēn	昏	2	jiǎu	狡	6
huēn	婚	20	jiē	階	20
húng	洪	8	jié	傑	9

jiè	藉	2
jiè	戒	20
jìn	燼	9
jǐng	井	8
jìng	競	3
jìng	勁	7
jiòu	舊	5
jiù	俱	12
jiù	懼	18
jiué	嚼	7
jiué	訣	12
jòu	宙	8
jr̀	置	7
jǔ	煮	19
juǎ	爪	18
juān	磚	12
juàn	撰	19
juāng	莊	15
juěn	准	9
jūng	鐘	16
jùng	重	3

K

káng	扛	7
kē	蚵	8
kū	窟	6
kuēn	昆	18
kùng	控	11
kuò	擴	11

L

lài	癩	20
lán	婪	6
lán	欄	8
làn	爛	11
léi	雷	16
lèng	愣	8
lì	粒	4
lì	立	6
lì	勵	16
lián	憐	1
liàn	潋	14
liáng	樑	14
liáng	糧	18
liǎng	倆	7
liàng	輛	8
liě	咧	6
lín	燐	10
lín	淋	16
líng	靈	16
liǒu	柳	14
liú	驢	7
lòu	露	6
lù	碌	15
luǎn	卵	1
lúng	龍	17
luó	羅	6

M

附錄三

má	麻	4	pén	盆	16	
má	蟆	10	pēng	烹	19	
māu	貓	17	péng	蓬	18	
méi	梅	20	pì	屁	7	
méng	濛	14	piān	篇	14	
mǐn	憫	1	piān	翩	15	
miòu	謬	7	pīn	拼	12	
mō	摸	14	pín	貧	12	
mǒ	抹	14	pō	坡	5	
mò	毛	5	pó	婆	11	
móu	謀	12	pǒu	剖	1	
mù	慕	8	pú	蹼	10	
mù	墓	10	pù	瀑	16	
mù	牧	11				

N

				R		
			rǎng	嚷	3	
nǐ	擬	11	rǎu	擾	18	
nián	黏	12	rě	惹	7	
niáng	娘	19	rèn	飪	19	
níng	凝	20	rēng	扔	13	
niuè	虐	7	róu	柔	2	
nù	怒	11	ruǎn	軟	7	
núng	濃	14				

O

				S		
			sǎ	撒	2	
ǒu	偶	10	shā	砂	4	
			shāng	湯	16	
P			shé	蛇	18	
pá	扒	9	shēn	伸	4	
pàn	判	11	shēng	生	5	

shēng	聲	6		sú	俗	20
shēng	牲	7		suèi	碎	11
shī	稀	11		suèi	穗	18
shí	惜	3		suěn	損	18
shiā	蝦	12		sūng	松	10
shiān	仙	4		sūng	鬆	17
shiān	掀	9				
shián	嫻	2		**T**		
shián	嫌	4		tái	抬	7
shián	絃	16		tān	貪	4
shiàn	羨	8		tǎn	毯	17
shiáng	翔	3		tàn	探	4
shiāu	逍	6		tau	桃	14
shiè	瀉	16		téng	疼	7
shíng	刑	12		téng	騰	17
shǐng	醒	11		tī	梯	16
shìng	杏	13		tí	堤	14
shiōu	繡	2		tíng	亭	20
shiòu	秀	3		tōu	偷	12
shiù	畜	11		tsāi	猜	9
shiún	巡	17		tsǎi	彩	4
shr̄	濕	9		tsáng	藏	2
shr̄	詩	14		tsū	粗	7
shr̄	獅	18		tsù	簇	18
shū	輸	19		tsuàn	竄	17
shū	抒	19		tsuèi	脆	7
shǔ	屬	15		tsúng	叢	6
shǔ	鼠	17		tsuò	措	7
sōu	搜	3		tsuò	撮	18
sū	蘇	14		tsž	此	1

附　錄　三　263

tù	兔	6	yàn	豔	2
tuǒ	妥	7	yàn	雁	10
tz̄	滋	1	yàn	灔	14
tź	姿	3	yáng	揚	16
tź	資	12	yāu	吆	7
tzàn	贊	14	yáu	遙	6
tzāng	臟	12	yǎu	咬	17
tzàng	葬	10	yǐ	尾	10
tzòu	奏	16	yì	藝	9
tzuàn	鑽	9	yì	翼	18
tzūng	蹤	17	yīn	姻	20
			yín	吟	14
	W		yīng	鷹	15
wǎ	瓦	12	yíng	螢	10
wán	玩	8	yíng	贏	19
wǎn	婉	3	yú	俞	16
wàng	忘	13	yú	渝	20
wéi	唯	10	yǔ	宇	8
wéi	巍	16	yù	獄	12
wěi	違	12	yù	欲	14
wěi	萎	10	yùn	蘊	12
wèi	偽	9	yǔng	擁	11
wū	烏	8			
wú	吳	20			
wù	惡	11			
	Y				
yān	淹	20			
yán	鹽	5			
yǎn	衍	18			

附錄四　本冊生字與生詞索引
（阿拉伯數字代表課數）

A

āhā	啊哈	ㄚ ㄏㄚ	an expression the same in pronunciation and meaning as the English "Ah ha!"	7
ānwèi	安慰	ㄢ ㄨㄟˋ	to console; to comfort; to soothe	16
àn	岸	ㄢˋ	the bank (of a river), the coast (of the sea)	8
àurán chāusú	傲然超俗	ㄠˋ ㄖㄢˊ ㄔㄠ ㄙㄨˊ	Haughty bone and free from vulgarity; uncommonly proud hearted and afraid of nothing	20

B

bàle	罷了	ㄅㄚˋ·ㄌㄜ	merely; only	5
bǎi	擺	ㄅㄞˇ	to aryrange; to display; to place; to be arranged; placed, etc.	5
bǎi	柏	ㄅㄞˇ	cypress	10
bàiguāng	敗光	ㄅㄞˋ ㄍㄨㄤ	used up and wasted	11
bāngwǎn	傍晚	ㄅㄤ ㄨㄢˇ	dusk; twilight.	17
bǎng	綁	ㄅㄤˇ	to tie; to bind	7
bǎu	飽	ㄅㄠˇ	to be full (stomach)	14
bàuyuàn	抱怨	ㄅㄠˋ ㄩㄢˋ	to complain; to grumble	3
bēishāng	悲傷	ㄅㄟ ㄕㄤ	sad; sorrowful; sadness	20

bēnfàng	奔放	ㄅㄣ ㄈㄤˋ	(said of writing emotions, etc) expressive and unrestrained; moving and forceful	16
běnchián	本錢	ㄅㄣˇ ㄑㄧㄢˊ	capital; investment	1
běnlǐng	本領	ㄅㄣˇ ㄌㄧㄥˇ	talent; ability; skill	3
běnshìng	本性	ㄅㄣˇ ㄒㄧㄥˋ	the real nature; natural character	15
běnjēn	本真	ㄅㄣˇ ㄓㄣ	real self; the real look; single and sincere	17
bēngtā	崩塌	ㄅㄥ ㄊㄚ	to collapse	17
bèngbèng tiàutiàu	蹦蹦跳跳	ㄅㄥˋ ㄅㄥˋ ㄊㄧㄠˋ ㄊㄧㄠˋ	skipping; romping; jumping; frolicing	6
bǐsài	比賽	ㄅㄧˇ ㄙㄞˋ	a contest; a match; a tournament; to compete in a contest, etc	19
bì	避	ㄅㄧˋ	to avoid; to evade; to hide	6
bìshià	陛下	ㄅㄧˋ ㄒㄧㄚˋ	Your Majesty	9
bìhuà	壁畫	ㄅㄧˋ ㄏㄨㄚˋ	a mural; a fresco	9
biǎuyǎn	表演	ㄅㄧㄠˇ ㄧㄢˇ	to perform; performance	3
biǎushr̀	表示	ㄅㄧㄠˇ ㄕˋ	to indicate; to show	4
biēsž	憋死	ㄅㄧㄝ ㄙˇ	to die from suffocation; to feel (a situation) is extremely stifling	13
biēchì	憋氣	ㄅㄧㄝ ㄑㄧˋ	to suffer a breathing obstruction; to hold your breath	13
bódé	博得	ㄅㄛˊ ㄉㄜˊ	to obtain; to win	3
bóhǎi	渤海	ㄅㄛˊ ㄏㄞˇ	the gulf between Liáu-dūng and Shān-dūng peninsulas	8
bó	薄	ㄅㄛˊ	thin; light	9

bótz	脖子	ㄅㄛˊ·ㄗ	the neck	10
bódòu	搏鬥	ㄅㄛˊ ㄉㄡˋ	to fight and struggle	18
bùgǎn	不敢	ㄅㄨˋ ㄍㄢˇ	dare not	2
bùshí	不惜	ㄅㄨˋ ㄒㄧˊ	at all costs; at any costs without regard to the price or consequences	3
bùrú	不如	ㄅㄨˋ ㄖㄨˊ	not as good as	3
bùshiànghuà	不像話	ㄅㄨˊ ㄒㄧㄤˋ ㄏㄨㄚˋ	outside normal and acceptable social behavior; too rediculous	7
bùshiāushūo	不消說	ㄅㄨˋ ㄒㄧㄠ ㄕㄨㄛ	it goes without saying	9
bùhé shŕyí	不合時宜	ㄅㄨˋ ㄏㄜˊ ㄕˊ ㄧˊ	be out of keeping with the times; be incompatible with present needs; be out of keeping with the objective conditions.	14
bùyǐ wéirán	不以爲然	ㄅㄨˋ ㄧˇ ㄨㄟˊ ㄖㄢˊ	object to; not approve; it take exception to…	14
bùbìwèi shēnggāu shìng,wèi szˇbēi shāng	不必爲生高興，爲死悲傷	ㄅㄨˋ ㄅㄧˋ ㄨㄟˋ ㄕㄥ ㄍㄠ ㄒㄧㄥˋ ㄨㄟˋ ㄙˇ ㄅㄟ ㄕㄤ	It's not necessary to be happy because of life, or sad because of death (ie. life and death are natural)	15
bǔjuō	捕捉	ㄅㄨˇ ㄓㄨㄛ	to catch	17
bù	佈	ㄅㄨˋ	to cover ; to arrange	20

C

chā	插	ㄔㄚ	to insert ; to plant	15

chāyāng	插秧	ㄔㄚ ㄧㄤ	transplanting rice seedlings	15
chāhuā	插花	ㄔㄚ ㄏㄨㄚ	to arrange flowers; flower arrangement	19
chāikāi	拆開	ㄔㄞ ㄎㄞ	to separate; to take apart; to open (a letter, box, etc.)	5
chǎnshēng	產生	ㄔㄢˇ ㄕㄥ	to be brought about; to give rise to; to produce	10
chángshēngbùlǎu	長生不老	ㄔㄤˊ ㄕㄥ ㄅㄨˋ ㄌㄠˇ	immortality and eternal youth	4
chángtí	長堤	ㄔㄤˊ ㄊㄧ	a long dike	14
cháng jiǎu	長角	ㄔㄤˊ ㄐㄧㄠˇ	long horns	18
chángchīng	常青	ㄔㄤˊ ㄑㄧㄥ	ever green	10
chēliàng	車輛	ㄔㄜ ㄌㄧㄤˋ	vehicles	8
chèntzǎu	趁早	ㄔㄣˋ ㄗㄠˇ	(to act) before it is too late; as early as possible	11
chèn	趁	ㄔㄣˋ	to take advantage of; to avail oneself of	11
chēng	撐	ㄔㄥ	to pole (a boat); to punt	19
chéng chi ānshàng wàn	成千上萬	ㄔㄥˊ ㄑㄧㄢ ㄕㄤˋ ㄨㄢˋ	countless; numerous; hundreds upon thousands; tens of thousands	8
chīhsiánchín	七絃琴	ㄑㄧ ㄒㄧㄢˊ ㄑㄧㄣˊ	a seven-stringed Chinese musical instrument	16
chíshŕ	其實	ㄑㄧˊ ㄕˊ	actually; in fact	12
chí	奇	ㄑㄧˊ	rare; special; wonderful	14
chǐhsiān	起先	ㄑㄧˇ ㄒㄧㄢ	in the beginning; at first	7
chǐbúshŕ	豈不是	ㄑㄧˇ ㄅㄨˊ	How could it not be; wouldn't	

		ㄕˋ	that be	14
chìyè	企業	ㄑㄧˋ ㄧㄝˋ	enterprise; business	11
chiàdāng	恰當	ㄑㄧㄚˋ ㄉㄤˋ	appropriate; fitting	10
chiánwǎng	前往	ㄑㄧㄢˊ ㄨㄤˇ	to visit; to go to (a place)	5
chiángbì	牆壁	ㄑㄧㄤˊ ㄅㄧˋ	the wall (of a building)	9
chiāují	敲擊	ㄑㄧㄠ ㄐㄧˊ	to beat; to knock	16
chiáu liáng	橋樑	ㄑㄧㄠˊ ㄌㄧㄤˊ	a bridge	14
chiàuchū	翹出	ㄑㄧㄠˋ ㄔㄨ	to stick up, out of, or across	18
chiǎu	巧	ㄑㄧㄠˇ	clever; ingenious; skillful	3
chiǎushé	巧舌	ㄑㄧㄠˇ ㄕㄜˊ	eloquent; glib	3
chiǎumiàu	巧妙	ㄑㄧㄠˇ ㄇㄧㄠˋ	ingenious; skillful	3
chiàubì	峭壁	ㄑㄧㄠˋ ㄅㄧˋ	a vertical cliff; a precipice	16
chièshŕ	切實	ㄑㄧㄝˋ ㄕˊ	sure; certain; thorough	6
chīn	親	ㄑㄧㄣ	to be intimate with; to be close to	10
chīnjìn	親近	ㄑㄧㄣ ㄐㄧㄣˋ	to get close; intimate	2
chīnmì	親密	ㄑㄧㄣ ㄇㄧˋ	to be close to; to be intimate with	10
chīngpén dàyǔ	傾盆大雨	ㄑㄧㄥ ㄆㄣˊ ㄉㄚˋ ㄩˇ	heavy rain; pouring	16
chín	琴	ㄑㄧㄣˊ	a musical instrument (usually stringed)	16
chínláu	勤勞	ㄑㄧㄣˊ ㄌㄠˊ	diligent; industrious; hard working	18
chīngwā	青蛙	ㄑㄧㄥ ㄨㄚ	a frog	6
chīngkuài	輕快	ㄑㄧㄥ ㄎㄨㄞˋ	sprightly; lightly; agile; brisk; lively	15
chíngfāng	晴方好	ㄑㄧㄥˊ ㄈㄤ	perfectly clear and sunny	14

hǎu		ㄏㄠˇ		
chǐngjiàu	請教	ㄑㄧㄥˇ ㄐㄧㄠˋ	to request instructions or advice	10
chióujiòu	求救	ㄑㄧㄡˊ ㄐㄧㄡˋ	to seek relief ; to ask for rescue or help	6
chióurén bùrú chióují	求人不如求己	ㄑㄧㄡˊ ㄖㄣˊ ㄅㄨˋ ㄖㄨˊ ㄑㄧㄡˊ ㄐㄧˇ	asking others for help is not as good as asking onesslf	6
chióu	球	ㄑㄧㄡˊ	a ball ; a sphere	8
chīu	曲	ㄑㄩ	to bend ; bend ; winding ; crooked	7
chīu	區	ㄑㄩ	an area, district or zone	14
chǐu	曲	ㄑㄩˇ	a piece of music ; measure word for a piece of music	16
chǐu	娶	ㄑㄩˇ	to take a wife	11
chiùwèi	趣味	ㄑㄩˋ ㄨㄟˋ	to be interesting	19
chiuàn	勸	ㄑㄩㄢˋ	to urge ; to exhort ; to caution ; to advise	2
chiuēdiǎn	缺點	ㄑㄩㄝ ㄉㄧㄢˇ	shortcoming ; defect ; flaw	14
chiuēshǎu	缺少	ㄑㄩㄝ ㄕㄠˇ	lacking ; deficient	19
chóuduàn	綢緞	ㄔㄡˊ ㄉㄨㄢˋ	silk goods	20
chr̄chr̄de	癡癡地	ㄔ ㄔ ˙ㄉㄜ	dazedly, in a mesmerized manner	2
chr̄lì	吃力	ㄔ ㄌㄧˋ	tired ; exhausted ; tiring and tough (work); take a lot of doing	7
chūyù	出獄	ㄔㄨ ㄩˋ	to get out of prison	12
chūrèn	出任	ㄔㄨ ㄖㄣˋ	to assume a position ; to take office	14

chúchiu	除去	ㄔㄨˊ ㄑㄩˋ	to get rid of	9
chúhuò	除禍	ㄔㄨˊ ㄏㄨㄛˋ	to get rid of trouble and ruin	11
chútz	廚子	ㄔㄨˊ·ㄗ	a cook	5
chǔli	處理	ㄔㄨˇ ㄌㄧˇ	to deal with; to handle	7
chǔtzài	處在	ㄔㄨˇ ㄗㄞˋ	living in; situated in	8
chùfàn shíngfǎ	觸犯刑法	ㄔㄨˋ ㄈㄢˋ ㄒㄧㄥˊ ㄈㄚˇ	to violate criminal law	12
chùshēng	畜生	ㄔㄨˋ ㄕㄥ	dumb creatures; cruel animal	13
chuǎng	闖	ㄔㄨㄤˇ	to rush into; to intrude into	12
chuǎng kūngmén	闖空門	ㄔㄨㄤˇ ㄎㄨㄥ ㄇㄣˊ	to intrude into an unguarded house for the purpose of stealing	12
chuàng tzuò	創作	ㄔㄨㄤˋ ㄗㄨㄛˋ	to create (an original work of literature or art); an original work of literature or art	16
chuàngtzàu	創造	ㄔㄨㄤˋ ㄗㄠˋ	to create	18
chūngshǐ	沖洗	ㄔㄨㄥ ㄒㄧˇ	to wash with running water	18
chǔngài	寵愛	ㄔㄨㄥˇ ㄞˋ	to favour or patronize; to dote on; favourite	9

D

dāchéng	搭乘	ㄉㄚ ㄔㄥˊ	to ride in (a train, bus, airplane, etc)	2
dāying	答應	ㄉㄚ ㄧㄥˋ	to promise; to assent to (a request)	5
dǎ	打	ㄉㄚˇ	to give (a grade, discount, etc)	14
dǎmài cháng	打麥場	ㄉㄚˇ ㄇㄞˋ ㄔㄤˊ	a place for threshing wheat or barley	9

dàfán	大凡	ㄉㄚˋ ㄈㄢˊ	generally speaking; ordinarily	16
dàyì	大翼	ㄉㄚˋ ㄧˋ	big wings	18
dài	待	ㄉㄞˋ	to treat; to entertain; to wait	3
dàiyù	待遇	ㄉㄞˋ ㄩˋ	pay; salary; treatment	3
dānbǎu	擔保	ㄉㄢ ㄅㄠˇ	to guarantee; a guarantee	18
dànjuāng núngmǒ	淡粧濃抹	ㄉㄢˋ ㄓㄨㄤ ㄋㄨㄥˊ ㄇㄛˇ	heavy or light makeup	14
dànshēng	誕生	ㄉㄢˋ ㄕㄥ	birth; be born	15
dǎngjù	擋住	ㄉㄤˇ ㄓㄨˋ	to block; to obstruct; to impede	17
dàu	倒	ㄉㄠˋ	to invert; to turn upside down; to put in neverse	7
dàulǐ	道理	ㄉㄠˋ ㄌㄧˇ	reason; rationality; sensible	1
dàutz	稻子	ㄉㄠˋ·ㄗ	unhulled rice	18
dàugǔ	稻穀	ㄉㄠˋ ㄍㄨˇ	rice kernel	18
dàusuěi	稻穗	ㄉㄠˋ ㄙㄨㄟˋ	the ear or spike of the rice plant	18
dàuchù	到處	ㄉㄠˋ ㄔㄨˋ	everywhere; all places	15
díchiuè	的確	ㄉㄧˊ ㄑㄩㄝˋ	certainly; surely	11
dìdàu	地道	ㄉㄧˋ ㄉㄠˋ	a tunnel	6
dìchióu	地球	ㄉㄧˋ ㄑㄧㄡˊ	the planet earth	8
dìlì	地利	ㄉㄧˋ ㄌㄧˋ	land productivity	12
dìtǎn	地毯	ㄉㄧˋ ㄊㄢˇ	a rug; a carpet	17
déyì yángyáng	得意洋洋	ㄉㄜˊ ㄧˋ ㄧㄤˊ ㄧㄤˊ	complacent (ly); feeling so satisfied with oneself; the air of one who feels (sometimes	8

附　錄　四　273

			unwarranted) great satisfaction, pride and pleasure at his own personality, accomplishments, or situation	
détzuèi	得罪	ㄉㄜˊㄗㄨㄟ	to offend	14
dēnglúng	燈籠	ㄉㄥ ㄉㄨㄥˊ	a lantern	10
dèngje	瞪着	ㄉㄥ˙ㄓㄜ	to stare at; to rivet one's gaze on…	2
dīdīdādā	滴滴答答	ㄉㄧ ㄉㄧ ㄉㄚ ㄉㄚ	The pitter patter of rain	16
diǎnshrchéng jīn	點石成金	ㄉㄧㄢˇ ㄕˊ ㄔㄥˊ ㄐㄧㄣ	Touch a stone and turn it into gold.	4
diǎn	點	ㄉㄧㄢˇ	to light; to ignite	9
diāu	雕	ㄉㄧㄠ	to engrave	3
diàuchá	調查	ㄉㄧㄠˋ ㄔㄚˊ	to investigate; to probe; to survey; an investigation	13
diàutz	調子	ㄉㄧㄠˋ˙ㄗ	a tune; a melody	16
dié	碟	ㄉㄧㄝˊ	a small plate	5
dǐng	頂	ㄉㄧㄥˇ	to carry on head; to prop up; to take our (responsibility); topmost; extremely; very.	1
dú	毒	ㄉㄨˊ	poison; toxin; harm; malice; to poison; poisonous; malicious	9
dújì	毒計	ㄉㄨˊ ㄐㄧˋ	a malicious plan	9
dúshé	毒蛇	ㄉㄨˊ ㄕㄜˊ	venomous snake(s)	18
dùhuà	度化	ㄉㄨˋ ㄏㄨㄚˋ	to deliver (someone) to a higher realm	4
dù	渡	ㄉㄨˋ	to cross (a river or ocean)	18

			; to pass through (a stage, time, a check point)	
duān	端	ㄉㄨㄢ	to hold sth. level with both hands	5
duēi	堆	ㄉㄨㄟ	to heap up ; to pile ; a heap ; a pile crowd	9
duèifāng	對方	ㄉㄨㄟˋㄈㄤ	the other side or party	9
duèishǒu	對手	ㄉㄨㄟˋㄕㄡˇ	an opponent	19
duèidá	對答	ㄉㄨㄟˋㄉㄚˊ	to give an answer ; to reply	19
duēn	蹲	ㄉㄨㄣ	to squat ; to crouch	18
dùngrén	動人	ㄉㄨㄥˋㄖㄣˊ	moving (as in feelings, emotions)	3
dùngjiāng	凍僵	ㄉㄨㄥˋㄐㄧㄤ	to be frozen stiff	20
duǒduǒ tsángtsáng	躲躲藏藏	ㄉㄨㄛˇㄉㄨㄛˇ ㄘㄤˊㄘㄤˊ	to hide ; to avoid	2

E

é	鵝	ㄜˊ	a goose ; geese	10
ēn-ēnaìaì	恩恩愛愛	ㄣㄣㄞˋㄞˋ	loving and devoted (said of a couple)	10
ěrduōruǎn	耳朵軟	ㄦˇㄉㄨㄛㄖㄨㄢˇ	gullible ; credulous ; easily convinced ; tending to believe too readily	7

F

fāguāng	發光	ㄈㄚㄍㄨㄤ	to emit light ; to shine ; to glitter.	10
fātsái	發財	ㄈㄚㄘㄞˊ	to become rich	11

fájīn	罰金	ㄈㄚˊ ㄐㄧㄣ	a fine ; to impose a fine.	12
fǎshù	法術	ㄈㄚˇ ㄕㄨˋ	an uncanny, occult, or supernatural feat; magic skills	4
fǎyuàn	法院	ㄈㄚˇ ㄩㄢˋ	a court of law	11
fǎguān	法官	ㄈㄚˇ ㄍㄨㄢ	a judge (of a court)	11
fānliǎn	翻臉	ㄈㄢ ㄌㄧㄢˇ	to turn hostile, to get angry ; to show displeasure	13
fānbiàn	翻遍	ㄈㄢ ㄆㄧㄢˋ	to turn through all (the pages of a book, etc)	19
fánrén	凡人	ㄈㄢˊ ㄖㄣˊ	an ordinary person ; one of the masses ; a mortal	4
fányǎn	繁衍	ㄈㄢˊ ㄧㄢˇ	proliferate.	18
fǎnbó	反駁	ㄈㄢˇ ㄅㄛˊ	to refute ; to rebut ; to dispute	14
fēishiāng	飛翔	ㄈㄟ ㄒㄧㄤˊ	to fly ; to hover	3
fēiyáng	飛揚	ㄈㄟ ㄧㄤˊ	to rise up and flutter (as a flag) ; to fly about	16
fēiténg	飛騰	ㄈㄟ ㄊㄥˊ	to fly high	17
fēnfēi	紛飛	ㄈㄣ ㄈㄟ	to fly all over ; to whirl around in confusion	20
fénshiāng	焚香	ㄈㄣˊ ㄒㄧㄤ	to burn incense (in worship, offering, etc)	16
fěn	粉	ㄈㄣˇ	powder ; flour	11
fěnsuèi	粉碎	ㄈㄣˇ ㄙㄨㄟˋ	to smash ; completely smashed	11
fēngjǐng chiū	風景區	ㄈㄥ ㄐㄧㄥˇ ㄑㄩ	scenic area.	14
fèng	縫	ㄈㄥˋ	a crack ; an opening ; a fis-	15

			sure	
fēngyī	縫衣	ㄈㄥˊㄧ	to sew ; sewing	19
fū	孵	ㄈㄨ	to hatch; to emerge from eggs or spawn	11
fūfù	夫婦	ㄈㄨ ㄈㄨˋ	husband and wife ; married couple	1
fūchī	夫妻	ㄈㄨ ㄑㄧ	a married couple ; husband and wife	10
fú	浮	ㄈㄨˊ	to float	17
fúyún	浮雲	ㄈㄨˊㄩㄣˊ	floating cloud	17
fújiàn	福建	ㄈㄨˊㄐㄧㄢˋ	Fú-jiàn Province	19
fù	婦	ㄈㄨˋ	a woman ; a wife ; a married woman	1
fùtzú	富足	ㄈㄨˋㄗㄨˊ	rich ; wealthy; abundant	1
fùwēng	富翁	ㄈㄨˋㄨㄥ	a rich man	1
fùbù	腹部	ㄈㄨˋㄅㄨˋ	the belly ; the abdomen	14

G

gaìshàng	蓋上	ㄍㄞˋㄕㄤ	to cover	9
gāntsueì	乾脆	ㄍㄢ ㄘㄨㄟˋ	might as well ; forward straight	7
gǎn	趕	ㄍㄢˇ	to make a dash for; to pursue ; to catch up ; to hurry ; to rush	2
gǎnjǐn	趕緊	ㄍㄢˇㄐㄧㄣˇ	quickly ; with no loss of time	7
gǎntzuò gǎnweí	敢做敢爲	ㄍㄢˇㄗㄨㄛˋ ㄍㄢˇㄨㄟˊ	venture to do and dare to act; take ones' courage in both hands	3

gǎnrén	感人	ㄍㄢˇ ㄖㄣˊ	moving ; touching	16
gāngliè	剛烈	ㄍㄤ ㄌㄧㄝˋ	tough and vehement; violent; strong and hot tempered	2
gāugāu shìng shìng	高高興興	ㄍㄠ ㄍㄠ ㄒㄧㄥˋ ㄒㄧㄥˋ	Highly elated and delighted	5
gāuming	高明	ㄍㄠ ㄇㄧㄥˊ	clever ; wise ; superior	16
gàutsź	告辭	ㄍㄠˋ ㄘˊ	to take leave ; to say good-bye (formal)	5
gējr̀	擱置	ㄍㄜ ㄓˋ	to shelve or pigeonhole (a plan, proposal, etc)	7
gēn	根	ㄍㄣ	measure word for things of slender shape, such as a stick, spear, a piece of string, rope, etc	7
gēnběn	根本	ㄍㄣ ㄅㄣˇ	root; base; origin; basically; at all; simply	10
gènggāu yiděng	更高一等	ㄍㄥˋ ㄍㄠ ㄧˋ ㄉㄥˇ	even better	17
gēngjùng	耕種	ㄍㄥ ㄓㄨㄥˋ	to plough and sow	12
gǒu	狗	ㄍㄡˇ	a dog	18
gòu	購	ㄍㄡˋ	to buy ; to purchase	3
gū-niang	姑娘	ㄍㄨ·ㄋㄧㄤ	an unmarried girl	19
gǔlì	鼓勵	ㄍㄨˇ ㄌㄧˋ	to encourage ; encouragement	16
gùdìng	固定	ㄍㄨˋ ㄉㄧㄥˋ	fixed; firm; to fix	1
gùyì	故意	ㄍㄨˋ ㄧˋ	on purpose; intentionally	17
gùyùng	僱用	ㄍㄨˋ ㄩㄥˋ	to hire ; to employ	3
guā	颳	ㄍㄨㄚ	to blow	17

guāguājiàu	聒聒叫	ㄍㄨㄚ ㄐㄧㄠ	very good; wonderful; excellent	19
guà	掛	ㄍㄨㄚˋ	to hang; to suspend	16
guài	怪	ㄍㄨㄞˋ	very	3
guānguāng	觀光	ㄍㄨㄢ ㄍㄨㄤ	to go sightseeing; sightseeing	1
guǎnlǐ	管理	ㄍㄨㄢˇ ㄌㄧˇ	to manage; to handle	3
guàn	灌	ㄍㄨㄢˋ	to pour; to fill	5
guànmù	灌木	ㄍㄨㄢˋ ㄇㄨˋ	shrubs	18
guāngtsǎi	光彩	ㄍㄨㄤ ㄘㄞˇ	luster; sheen-gloss	4
guǎngbó	廣博	ㄍㄨㄤˇ ㄅㄛˊ	wide; extensive (knowledge)	8
guēimó	規模	ㄍㄨㄟ ㄇㄛˊ	scale; magnitude; scope	11
guěn	滾	ㄍㄨㄣˇ	to roll	20
guěnchūchiù	滾出去	ㄍㄨㄣˇ ㄔㄨ ㄑㄩˋ	get lost; get out of here	20
gūngdiàn	宮殿	ㄍㄨㄥ ㄉㄧㄢˋ	a palace	9
gūng	公	ㄍㄨㄥ	a respectful term of address.	14
guōgūngfǔ	郭公甫	ㄍㄨㄛ ㄍㄨㄥ ㄈㄨˇ	a friend of Sū Dūng-pō (蘇東坡)	14
guǒrán	果然	ㄍㄨㄛˇ ㄖㄢˊ	as expected; exactly as one expected	4

H

hámá	蝦蟆	ㄏㄚˊ ˙ㄇㄚ	a toad	10
hǎiyáng	海洋	ㄏㄞˇ ㄧㄤˊ	the ocean	8
Hǎinán	海南	ㄏㄞˇ ㄋㄢˊ	Hǎi-nán Province	19
hàirénfǎnhàijǐ	害人反害己	ㄏㄞˋ ㄖㄣˊ ㄈㄢˇ ㄏㄞˋ ㄐㄧˇ	Harming others may turn to harm oneself (curses come	9

		ㄐㄧˇ	home to roost); one who wants to harm others, but ends up only harming himself	
handūng	寒冬	ㄏㄢˊ ㄉㄨㄥ	a cold winter	20
hángjōu	杭州	ㄏㄤˊ ㄓㄡ	Háng-jōu is situated in Jè Jiāng Province (浙江省).	14
háumáu	毫毛	ㄏㄠˊ ㄇㄠˊ	fine hair	8
hǎushǒu	好手	ㄏㄠˇ ㄕㄡˇ	an expert (involving some kind of manual skill); good hand; be adept at	3
hàu	號	ㄏㄠˋ	second name	14
hélǐ	合理	ㄏㄜˊ ㄌㄧˇ	reasonable; logical	13
hécháng	何嘗	ㄏㄜˊ ㄔㄤˊ	How (could it be an exception)	8
héping shiāng chǔ	和平相處	ㄏㄜˊ ㄆㄧㄥˊ ㄒㄧㄤ ㄔㄨˇ	get along peacefully; peaceful coexistence	18
hè	鶴	ㄏㄜˋ	a crane (bird)	10
hóutz	猴子	ㄏㄡˊ·ㄗ	a monkey	6
húdié	蝴蝶	ㄏㄨˊ ㄉㄧㄝˊ	butterfly	15
hútz	鬍子	ㄏㄨˊ·ㄗ	a beard.	20
hùshiāng	互相	ㄏㄨˋ ㄒㄧㄤ	mutually; reciprocally; each other	9
hùshiāng jìdù	互相嫉妒	ㄏㄨˋ ㄒㄧㄤ ㄐㄧˊ ㄉㄨˋ	mutual jealousy; jealousy of each other	9
huāguāng	花光	ㄏㄨㄚ ㄍㄨㄤ	use up (money)	1
huāhuā	花花世界	ㄏㄨㄚ	the gay and material world	8

shr̄jiè		ㄏㄨㄚ ㄕˋ ㄐㄧㄝˋ	the mortal world (The dazzling human world with its myriad temptations)	
huāduǒ	花朵	ㄏㄨㄚ ㄉㄨㄛˇ	flowers	15
huá	滑	ㄏㄨㄚˊ	to slip; to slide; slippery; cunning; insincere	14
huàchéng	化成	ㄏㄨㄚˋ ㄔㄥˊ	to transform into; to become,	20
huài	壞	ㄏㄨㄞˋ	broken; bad; mean	10
huānshīn	歡心	ㄏㄨㄢ ㄒㄧㄣ	(to win another's) favour or heart	3
huāng miòuwú jī	荒謬無稽	ㄏㄨㄤ ㄇㄧㄡˋ ㄨˊ ㄐㄧ	preposterous; absurd and unfounded; sheer nonsense	7
huāngyě	荒野	ㄏㄨㄤ ㄧㄝˇ	the wilderness	20
huáng huēn	黃昏	ㄏㄨㄤˊ ㄏㄨㄣ	dusk, twilight	2
huáng yīng	黃鶯	ㄏㄨㄤˊ ㄧㄥ	oriole(s)	15
huáng chéng chéngde	黃澄澄的	ㄏㄨㄤˊ ㄔㄥˊ ㄔㄥˊ ˙ㄉㄜ	golden yellow	4
huēijìn	灰燼	ㄏㄨㄟ ㄐㄧㄣˋ	ashes; embers.	9
huèishr̄	惠施	ㄏㄨㄟˋ ㄕ	a good friend of Juāng Tzˇ (莊子)	15
huēn-àn	昏暗	ㄏㄨㄣ ㄢˋ	dark; murky; hazy	16
huēnyīn	婚姻	ㄏㄨㄣ ㄧㄣ	marriage	20
húng shuěi	洪水	ㄏㄨㄥˊ ㄕㄨㄟˇ	flood; a deluge	8

húngyàn	紅豔	ㄏㄨㄥˊ ㄧㄢˋ	rich red	20
huògēn	禍根	ㄏㄨㄛˋ ㄍㄣ	root of trouble	11
huò	獲	ㄏㄨㄛˋ	to get; to obtain	12

J

já	紮	ㄓㄚˊ	to bind; to tie; to fasten	13
jān	沾	ㄓㄢ	to be stuck to or marked with	18
jǎn	盞	ㄓㄢˇ	measure word for lamps	10
jànwéi jǐyǒu	佔爲己有	ㄓㄢˋ ㄨㄟˊ ㄐㄧˇ ㄧㄡˇ	take forcible possession of…	12
jàn	佔	ㄓㄢˋ	to occupy; to usurp; to seize	12
jāudài	招待	ㄓㄠ ㄉㄞˋ	to receive; to welcome; to look after (a guest)	5
jāujiàn	召見	ㄓㄠˋ ㄐㄧㄢˋ	to summon (a subordinate); to be summoned (by a superior); a summons	9
jāukāi	召開	ㄓㄠˋ ㄎㄞ	to convene or call (a meeting)	18
jāuyún	朝雲	ㄓㄠ ㄩㄣˊ	the name of a concubine of Sū Dūng-pō (蘇東坡)	14
jējù	遮住	ㄓㄜ ㄓㄨˋ	to cover; to block	9
jēmò	遮沒	ㄓㄜ ㄇㄛˋ	to completely cover; to obscure	16
jèyīdiǎn	這一點	ㄓㄜˋ ㄧ ㄉㄧㄢˇ	this point	10
jēn	珍	ㄓㄣ	precious; rare; very valuable	3
jēnchín	珍禽	ㄓㄣ ㄑㄧㄣˊ	a rare bird	3
jēnlǐ	眞理	ㄓㄣ ㄌㄧˇ	the truth	10
jēngbiàn bùshià	爭辯不下	ㄓㄥ ㄅㄧㄢˋ ㄅㄨˋ ㄒㄧㄚˋ	to argue or debate without coming to a solution or re-	10

			sult; to sticks to his own stand	
jēngduó	爭奪	ㄓㄥ ㄉㄨㄛˊ	to struggle over; to scramble for; to contend for	18
jēngjá	掙扎	ㄓㄥ ㄓㄚˊ	to struggle or strive for; struggle	18
jèngchiuè	正確	ㄓㄥˋ ㄑㄩㄝˋ	accurate; correct	10
jèngdàu	正道	ㄓㄥˋ ㄉㄠˋ	the proper way; the right course	12
jèngjīng	正經	ㄓㄥˋ ㄐㄧㄥ	very proper; serious; decent; respectable	19
jīliè	激烈	ㄐㄧ ㄌㄧㄝˋ	heated (debate, battle, etc); drastic (measures, means, etc); violent (actions, speeches, etc); radical (party, etc)	16
jīáng	激昂	ㄐㄧ ㄤˊ	high-spirited; tremendously excited	16
jīyuè	激越	ㄐㄧ ㄩㄝˋ	sonorous; having a full, rich and deep sound	16
jīshiàu	譏笑	ㄐㄧ ㄒㄧㄠˋ	to ridicule; to laugh at; to make fun at	8
jījr̄	機智	ㄐㄧ ㄓˋ	alertness; wit; ready responsiveness	14
jì	技	ㄐㄧˋ	special ability; skill; ingenuity; dexterity	3
jìchéng	繼承	ㄐㄧˋ ㄔㄥˊ	to succeed to; to inherit	9
jìjié	季節	ㄐㄧˋ ㄐㄧㄝˊ	a season	12
jìtuō	寄託	ㄐㄧˋ ㄊㄨㄛ	to consign or commit (emo-	16

附　錄　四　283

jìdiàn	祭奠	ㄐㄧˋㄉㄧㄢˋ	tions to writing, soul to god, etc) to offer sacrifices to the spirit of a deceased person	16
jiākuān	加寬	ㄐㄧㄚㄎㄨㄢ	to broaden; to be widened	8
jiāyáu	佳肴	ㄐㄧㄚㄧㄠˊ	excellent food or dishes	5
jiǎshř	假使	ㄐㄧㄚˇㄕˇ	if; supposing	2
jiǎchúng	甲蟲	ㄐㄧㄚˇㄔㄨㄥˊ	a beetle	10
jiānbǎng	肩膀	ㄐㄧㄢㄅㄤˇ	the shoulder(s)	7
jiānchiáng	堅強	ㄐㄧㄢㄑㄧㄤˊ	strong; firm; unyielding	10
jiānshŕ	堅實	ㄐㄧㄢㄕˊ	solid; strong; durable	10
jiānjēn búyú	堅貞不渝	ㄐㄧㄢㄓㄣㄅㄨˋㄩˊ	unyielding; unchanging faithfulness	20
jiānkǔ	艱苦	ㄐㄧㄢㄎㄨˇ	trying and hard; hardship	18
jiānyá	尖牙	ㄐㄧㄢㄧㄚˊ	sharp teeth	18
jiāngù	兼顧	ㄐㄧㄢㄍㄨˋ	to take care of the needs, etc. of two things or parties	18
jiàntzàu	建造	ㄐㄧㄢˋㄗㄠˋ	to build; to construct	3
jiànjúshī	建築師	ㄐㄧㄢˋㄓㄨˊㄕ	an architect	9
jiànwén	見聞	ㄐㄧㄢˋㄨㄣˊ	one's experience (of life); what one has seen and heard; general knowledge	8
jiànshŕ chiǎnbó	見識淺薄	ㄐㄧㄢˋㄕˊㄑㄧㄢˇㄅㄛˊ	superficial knowledge and experience	8
jiànshǎng	鑑賞力	ㄐㄧㄢˋ	powers of discernment and ap-	16

lì		ㄕㄤˇ ㄌㄧˋ	preciation (as a connoisseur might have)	
jiāngběn chióulì	將本求利	ㄐㄧㄤ ㄅㄣˇ ㄑㄧㄡˊ ㄌㄧˋ	(Lit) with using capital to earn profit	1
jiǎutù sānkū	狡兔三窟	ㄐㄧㄠˇ ㄊㄨˋ ㄙㄢ ㄎㄨ	A cunning rabbit has three exits (as it's burrow)	6
jiǎuhuá	狡滑	ㄐㄧㄠˇ ㄏㄨㄚˊ	cunning; sly; crafty	18
jiàurǎng	叫嚷	ㄐㄧㄠˋ ㄖㄤˇ	shout, make a great noise	3
jiàushǐng	叫醒	ㄐㄧㄠˋ ㄒㄧㄥˇ	to waken	11
jiàu	叫	ㄐㄧㄠˋ	to let; to make	17
jiēchù	接觸	ㄐㄧㄝ ㄔㄨˋ	to make contact with; to come in contact with	9
jiē	階	ㄐㄧㄝ	steps; stairs	20
jiéchū	傑出	ㄐㄧㄝˊ ㄔㄨ	outstanding; eminent	9
jiéyù	節育	ㄐㄧㄝˊ ㄩˋ	birth control; to practice birth control	18
jié	結	ㄐㄧㄝˊ	to bear fruit	13
jiě	姊	ㄐㄧㄝˇ	elder sister	2
jiěmèi	姊妹	ㄐㄧㄝˇ ㄇㄟˋ	sisters	2
jiègù	藉故	ㄐㄧㄝˋ ㄍㄨˋ	to use…as an excuse; to find an excuse for…	2
jiètz	戒子	ㄐㄧㄝˋ ˙ㄗ	a ring	20
jièyùng	借用	ㄐㄧㄝˋ ㄩㄥˋ	to borrow	5
jǐn	緊	ㄐㄧㄣˇ	tight; firm; secure; taut; tense	13
jǐnjāng	緊張	ㄐㄧㄣˇ ㄓㄤ	tense; nervous	15
jìnbù	進步	ㄐㄧㄣˋ ㄅㄨˋ	improvement; progress; advancement	3

jīngjř	精緻	ㄐㄧㄥ ㄓˋ	exquisite	5
jīngyà	驚訝	ㄐㄧㄥ ㄧㄚˋ	to be amazed; to be astonished; be surprised; be alarmed	8
jīngrǎu	驚擾	ㄐㄧㄥ ㄖㄠˇ	to disturb; to cause trouble to others; disturbed	18
jǐngdǐjr̄wā	井底之蛙	ㄐㄧㄥˇ ㄉㄧˇ ㄓ ㄨㄚ	the frog at the bottom of the well; a person of limited outlook and experience	8
jìngjēng	競爭	ㄐㄧㄥˋ ㄓㄥ	competition; to compete	3
jìng	竟	ㄐㄧㄥˋ	rather unexpectedly; in a way thought to be rather unlikely	7
jièer	勁兒	ㄐㄧㄝˋㄦ	vigor; energy; enthusiasm	7
jìngjìn	淨盡	ㄐㄧㄥˋ ㄐㄧㄣˋ	completely exhausted (stocks, supplies, etc)	18
jiòu	舊	ㄐㄧㄡˋ	former; old; ancient	5
jiòurén yàujiòu dàudǐ	救人要救到底	ㄐㄧㄡˋㄖㄣˊ ㄧㄠˋㄐㄧㄡˋ ㄉㄠˋㄉㄧˇ	when saving somebody, save them completely	13
jiùyǒu	具有	ㄐㄩˋㄧㄡˇ	to have	11
jiuéduèi	絕對	ㄐㄩㄝˊ ㄉㄨㄟˋ	absolute; unconditional	10
jōu	洲	ㄓㄡ	a continent	8
jr̄	支	ㄓ	measure word for songs, incense, cigarettes, etc	1
jr̄chū	支出	ㄓ ㄔㄨ	expense; expenditure; to spend; to pay out	1
jr̄shr̄	知識	ㄓ ㄕˋ	knowledge	8
jr̄yīn	知音	ㄓ ㄧㄣ	a close friend who really understands you	16

jīyīn nánchióu	知音難求	ㄓ ㄧㄣ ㄋㄢˊ ㄑㄧㄡˊ	a bosom friend keenly appreciative of your talent is hard to find	16
jŕcháng tz	直腸子	ㄓˊ ㄔㄤˊ ˙ㄗ	out spoken; frank; blunt	14
jŕshuài	直率	ㄓˊ ㄕㄨㄞˋ	direct; frank; honest; blunt	14
jr̀huèi	智慧	ㄓˋ ㄏㄨㄟˋ	intelligence; wisdom	6
jr̀fù	致富	ㄓˋ ㄈㄨˋ	to become rich; to acquire wealth	12
jūhuā	珠花	ㄓㄨ ㄏㄨㄚ	hair decoration of pearl. a kind of pearl head ornament	1
jútz	竹子	ㄓㄨˊ ˙ㄗ	bamboo	14
jŭchá	煮茶	ㄓㄨˇ ㄔㄚˊ	to boil tea	19
jùjùng	注重	ㄓㄨˋ ㄓㄨㄥˋ	to emphasize; to attach importance to	20
juānwă	磚瓦	ㄓㄨㄢ ㄨㄚˇ	bricks and tiles	12
juānkàu	專靠	ㄓㄨㄢ ㄎㄠˋ	to specifically depend on	18
juànshiĕ	撰寫	ㄓㄨㄢˋ ㄒㄧㄝˇ	to write or compose	19
juāng	裝	ㄓㄨㄤ	to pack; to fill in or up	14
juāngtž	莊子	ㄓㄨㄤ ㄗˇ	姓莊名周 (Jōu). Famous Philosopher of the Warring States Period	15
juēi	追	ㄓㄨㄟ	to chase; to pursue; to follow	6
juēigēn jióudĭ	追根究底	ㄓㄨㄟ ㄍㄣ ㄐㄧㄡˋ ㄉㄧˇ	to get to the root and find the bottom; to get to the bottom of (something)	10
juěnbèi	準備	ㄓㄨㄣˇ	to prepare; to get ready; to	5

		ㄅㄟˇ	be prepared, etc	
juěnshiǔ	准許	ㄓㄨㄣˇ ㄒㄩˇ	to permit; to allow	9
jūngyāng	中央	ㄓㄨㄥ ㄧㄤ	the center	9
jūngtz̀-chí	鍾子期	ㄓㄨㄥ ㄗˇ ㄑㄧˊ	a friend of Yú Bó-yá and music lover	16
jūngshīn	忠心	ㄓㄨㄥ ㄒㄧㄣ	loyal; faithful; loyalty; faithfulness	18
jùngchóu	重酬	ㄓㄨㄥˋ ㄔㄡˊ	a substantial reward given in return for something; remuneration	3
jùngshr̀	重視	ㄓㄨㄥˋ ㄕˋ	to consider important; to attach much importance to	3
jùngtzuèi	重罪	ㄓㄨㄥˋ ㄗㄨㄟˋ	serious offense	11

K

kāifā	開發	ㄎㄞ ㄈㄚ	to develop; developed; development (of natural resources, industry, etc)	14
káng	扛	ㄎㄤˊ	to carry something heavy on the shoulder(s)	7
kēdǒu	蝌蚪	ㄎㄜ ㄉㄡˇ	a tadpole	8
kěwù	可惡	ㄎㄜˇ ㄨˋ	detestable; hateful; abhorrent	11
kǒutsái	口才	ㄎㄡˇ ㄘㄞˊ	eloquence	15
kǒuwèi	口味	ㄎㄡˇ ㄨㄟˋ	taste	19
kū	窟	ㄎㄨ	a hole; a cave; a pit; a den	6
kūwěi	枯萎	ㄎㄨ ㄨㄟˇ	be withered	10
kuēn	昆蟲	ㄎㄨㄣ	insects	18

chúng		ㄔㄨㄥˊ		
kuènkǔ	困苦	ㄎㄨㄣˋㄎㄨˇ	in great distress; poverty stricken	1
kūngméng	空濛	ㄎㄨㄥㄇㄥˊ	the misty atmosphere of rainy days	14
kūngfù	空腹	ㄎㄨㄥㄈㄨˋ	an empty stomach	5
kǔngjiù	恐懼	ㄎㄨㄥˇㄐㄩˋ	frightened; fear; dread	18
kùnggàu	控告	ㄎㄨㄥˋㄍㄠˋ	to sue; to accuse	11
kuòchūng	擴充	ㄎㄨㄛˋㄔㄨㄥ	to expand; expansion	11

L

láilái wǎngwǎng	來來往往	ㄌㄞˊㄌㄞˊㄨㄤˇㄨㄤˇ	coming and going (in great numbers)	8
làihama shiǎngchr tiānéròu	癩蝦蟆想吃天鵝肉	ㄌㄞˋㄏㄚˊ·ㄇㄚㄒㄧㄤˇㄔ ㄊㄧㄢㄜˊㄖㄡˋ	the ugly toad wants to eat swan meat (lit). refers to a male suitor who doesn't have the qualifications, or attributes to ask a woman for her hand in marriage	20
lángān	欄杆	ㄌㄢˊㄍㄢ	a railing	8
láu	勞	ㄌㄠˊ	to toil; to work	12
lǎuběn	老本	ㄌㄠˇㄅㄣˇ	the original investment; capital one's last stakes	1
lǎudiē	老爹	ㄌㄠˇㄉㄧㄝ	father; respectful address for an aged man	7
lǎupó	老婆	ㄌㄠˇㄆㄛˊ	a wife	11
lǎutóu	老頭子	ㄌㄠˇㄊㄡˊ	an old man	13

tz		˙ㄗ		
lǎushǔ	老鼠	ㄌㄠˇㄕㄨˇ	a rat; a mouse	17
lèyì	樂意	ㄌㄜˋㄧˋ	willing to; glad to	9
lǐluèn	理論	ㄌㄧˇㄌㄨㄣˋ	to argue; to reason; a theory	12
lìshí	利息	ㄌㄧˋㄒㄧˊ	interest	1
lìjuǎ	利爪	ㄌㄧˋㄓㄨㄚˇ	sharp claws	18
lì	粒	ㄌㄧˋ	a grain (measure word for rice, sand, etc); a pill; a bead	4
lìkè	立刻	ㄌㄧˋㄎㄜˋ	immediately	9
liánmǐn	憐憫	ㄌㄧㄢˊㄇㄧㄣˇ	to take pity on…; to feel or show sorrow or pity for; to sympathize with; merciful	1
liányè	連夜	ㄌㄧㄢˊㄧㄝˋ	all through the night	11
liǎnhúng erchř	臉紅耳赤	ㄌㄧㄢˇㄏㄨㄥˊㄦˇㄔˋ	face and ears turn red (blush with shame)	19
liànyàn	激艷	ㄌㄧㄢˋㄧㄢˋ	the movement and flowing of water	14
liángshŕ	糧食	ㄌㄧㄤˊㄕˊ	food stuff; provisions; grains	18
liǎng	倆	ㄌㄧㄤˇ	two people	7
liáutiān	聊天	ㄌㄧㄠˊㄊㄧㄢ	to chat with	5
liǎujiě	了解	ㄌㄧㄠˇㄐㄧㄝˇ	to understand; understanding	12
liǎubùchǐ	了不起	ㄌㄧㄠˇㄅㄨˋㄑㄧˇ	excellent; very good; incredible	8
liàulǐ hòushŕ	料理後事	ㄌㄧㄠˋㄌㄧˇㄏㄡˋㄕˋ	to take care of matters after a person's death; make arrangement for a funeral	9

liěkāi	咧開	ㄌㄧㄝˇ ㄎㄞ	to open the mouth wide	6
lièren	獵人	ㄌㄧㄝˋ ㄖㄣˊ	a hunter	13
línhuǒjiǎchung	燐火甲蟲	ㄌㄧㄣˊ ㄏㄨㄛˇ ㄐㄧㄚˇ ㄔㄨㄥˊ	a kind of light-emitting beetle	10
línjiū	鄰居	ㄌㄧㄣˊ ㄐㄩ	neighbour(s)	11
línyǔ	淋雨	ㄌㄧㄣˊ ㄩˇ	to get wet in the rain	16
língchiǎu	靈巧	ㄌㄧㄥˊ ㄑㄧㄠˇ	clever; dexterous	18
Lióu Gùngfǔ	劉貢父	ㄌㄧㄡˊ ㄍㄨㄥˋ ㄈㄨˇ	(1022-1088 A.D) A good friend of Sū Dūng-pō	5
lǐngwù	領悟	ㄌㄧㄥˇ ㄨˋ	to comprehend; to understand; to realize	5
lióusān-mèi	劉三妹	ㄌㄧㄡˊ ㄙㄢ ㄇㄟˋ	woman's name	19
liǒushù	柳樹	ㄌㄧㄡˇ ㄕㄨˋ	the willow tree	14
lǘ	驢	ㄌㄩˊ	a donkey	7
lǚyóu	旅遊	ㄌㄩˇ ㄧㄡˊ	to go touring	1
lòu	露	ㄌㄡˋ	to reveal; to emerge; to show	6
luéntz	輪子	ㄌㄨㄣˊ ˙ㄗ	a wheel	10
lúng	籠	ㄌㄨㄥˊ	a cage	3
lúng	龍	ㄌㄨㄥˊ	dragon	17
luóbo	蘿蔔	ㄌㄨㄛˊ ˙ㄅㄛ	a radish	5
LuóShioutsái	羅秀才	ㄌㄨㄛˊ ㄒㄧㄡˋ ㄘㄞˊ	a person's name	19

M

máfán	麻煩	ㄇㄚˊ ㄈㄢˊ	trouble; troublesome; a hassle.	4

mábù	麻布	ㄇㄚˊ ㄅㄨˋ	hemp cloth	13
màigǎn	麥桿	ㄇㄞˋ ㄍㄢˇ	stalks of wheat or barley	9
mánglù	忙碌	ㄇㄤˊ ㄌㄨˋ	busy and in great haste; fully occupied	15
māu	貓	ㄇㄠ	cat(s)	17
méiānhǎushīn	沒安好心	ㄇㄟˊ ㄢ ㄏㄠˇ ㄒㄧㄣ	to have bad intentions	13
méijé	沒轍	ㄇㄟˊ ㄓㄜˊ	no way or method (to do something)	17
méihuā	梅花	ㄇㄟˊ ㄏㄨㄚ	plum blossoms	20
měimiàu	美妙	ㄇㄟˇ ㄇㄧㄠˋ	exquisite; very pleasant	3
měitz chiǎushé	美姿巧舌	ㄇㄟˇ ㄗ ㄑㄧㄠˇ ㄕㄜˊ	beautiful in poise and bearing and eloquent in speech	3
mèi	妹	ㄇㄟˋ	younger sister	2
méndāng hùduèi	門當户對	ㄇㄣˊ ㄉㄤ ㄏㄨˋ ㄉㄨㄟˋ	The doors of both sides are well matched (marry with one's match); families of equal standing (usually referring to those of a married couple); well matched	20
měngshòu	猛獸	ㄇㄥˇ ㄕㄡˋ	fierce wild beasts	18
michiè	密切	ㄇㄧˋ ㄑㄧㄝˋ	close or intimate (of relations, contact, etc)	8
mì	密	ㄇㄧˋ	dense; intimate	20
mìjiué	祕訣	ㄇㄧˋ ㄐㄩㄝˊ	a knack; secrets (of success, etc); the key (to the solution of a problem)	12
mō	摸	ㄇㄛ	to feel or touch (with the fin	14

			gers)	
mò	毛	ㄇㄛˋ	In ancient China 「毛」 and 「沒」 both pronounced (ㄇㄛˋ ; mò), meant 沒有	5
móushēng	謀生	ㄇㄡˊㄕㄥ	to make a living	12
mùchái	木柴	ㄇㄨˋㄔㄞˊ	firewood	9
mù	墓	ㄇㄨˋ	a grave ; a tomb	10

N

náshǒu	拿手	ㄋㄚˊㄕㄡˇ	one's special skill or ability ; to be particularly good or dexterous at	19
nándé	難得	ㄋㄢˊㄉㄜˊ	rare ; hard to come by; seldom; rarely	4
nándǎo	難倒	ㄋㄢˊㄉㄠˇ	to baffle; be baffled; to put (somebody) into a situation where they can't answer a question, solve a problem, etc	15
nénggòu	能夠	ㄋㄥˊㄍㄡˋ	can; be able to ; capable of	1
néngyán shàndào	能言善道	ㄋㄥˊㄧㄢˊㄕㄢˋㄉㄠˋ	eloquent; have the gift of the gab; have a glib tongue (Lit.); able to speak and know how to say it properly; have a ready tongue	3
nǐ	擬	ㄋㄧˇ	to plan ; to intend ; to decide ; to determine	11
niánjì	年紀	ㄋㄧㄢˊㄐㄧˋ	a person's age	1
nián	黏	ㄋㄧㄢˊ	to stick ; sticky ; adhesive ; viscous	12

niántǔ	黏土	ㄋㄧㄢˊ ㄊㄨˇ	clay	12
níngjié	凝結	ㄋㄧㄥˊ ㄐㄧㄝˊ	to condense (gas to liquid); to solidify or congeal (liquid to solid)	20
nióutzǎi huáng	牛仔黃	ㄋㄧㄡˊ ㄗㄞˇ ㄏㄨㄤˊ	Cowboy Huáng (a name)	20
niuèdài	虐待	ㄋㄩㄝˋ ㄉㄞˋ	to maltreat; to torment	7
núngfū	農夫	ㄋㄨㄥˊ ㄈㄨ	farmer(s)	15

P

pá	扒	ㄆㄚˊ	to scratch; to claw; to dig up	9
pāi	拍	ㄆㄞ	to strike (with the hand); to slap; to pat	11
pàichiǎn	派遣	ㄆㄞˋ ㄑㄧㄢˇ	to dispatch; to assign; to be assigned; to be sent	9
PánGǔ	盤古	ㄆㄢˊ ㄍㄨˇ	the legendary creator and first ruler of the universe	18
pàn	判	ㄆㄢˋ	to judge; to convict	11
pànshíng	判刑	ㄆㄢˋ ㄒㄧㄥˊ	to sentence	12
pèiǒu	配偶	ㄆㄟˋ ㄡˇ	spouse	10
pēngrèn	烹飪	ㄆㄥ ㄖㄣˋ	to cook; cooking	19
péngbó	蓬勃	ㄆㄥˊ ㄅㄛˊ	prospering; flourishing	18
pěngfù dàshiàu	捧腹大笑	ㄆㄥˇ ㄈㄨˋ ㄉㄚˋ ㄒㄧㄠˋ	to split (hold) one's sides with laughter	14
pèngdàu	碰到	ㄆㄥˋ ㄉㄠˋ	to meet someone unexpectedly; to touch something	17
pìgǔ	屁股	ㄆㄧˋ ㄍㄨˇ	arse; butt; bum	7
piān	篇	ㄆㄧㄢ	measure word for poems, co-	14

			mpositions, etc	
piānpiān fēiwǔ	翩翩飛舞	ㄆㄧㄢ ㄆㄧㄢ ㄈㄟ ㄨˇ	to fly gracefully and lightly	15
pīnmìng	拼命	ㄆㄧㄣ ㄇㄧㄥˋ	going all out to do something, usually somewhat recklessly; for the sake of one's life; risk one's life	12
pīnhé	拼合	ㄆㄧㄣ ㄏㄜˊ	to join together; to put together; to make a whole	5
pínchiúng	貧窮	ㄆㄧㄣˊ ㄑㄩㄥˊ	poor	12
píngpàn	評判	ㄆㄧㄥˊ ㄆㄢˋ	to judge or decide (as in a contest); judgment, etc	13
pǒukāi	剖開	ㄆㄡˇ ㄎㄞ	to cut; to open	1
pú	蹼	ㄆㄨˊ	webs on the feet of water fowl	10
pùbù	瀑布	ㄆㄨˋ ㄅㄨˋ	waterfall	16

R

rě	惹	ㄖㄜˇ	to provoke; to rouse; to cause	7
rènau	熱鬧	ㄖㄜˋ ㄋㄠˋ	noisy and bustling (place)	8
rénjiàn rénài	人見人愛	ㄖㄣˊ ㄐㄧㄢˋ ㄖㄣˊ ㄞˋ	whoever see him (it) will like him (it); likeable	4
rénshuō dūngjiòu shiàng dūng, rénshuō	人說東就向東，人說西就向西	ㄖㄣˊ ㄕㄨㄛ ㄉㄨㄥ ㄐㄧㄡˋ ㄒㄧㄤˋ ㄉㄨㄥ，ㄖㄣˊ ㄕㄨㄛ ㄒㄧ	to do everything people tell you to do	7

shījiōu		ㄐㄧㄡˉㄒㄧㄤˋ		
shiàngshī		ㄒㄧ		
réntzāng	人贓俱獲	ㄖㄣˊㄗㄤ	a theif caught together with	12
jiùhuò		ㄐㄩˋㄏㄨㄛˋ	the loot	
rénching	人情	ㄖㄣˊㄑㄧㄥˊ	good will (expressed in the form of gifts, invitations, etc); favours asked or done	13
rěnshòu	忍受	ㄖㄣˇㄕㄡˋ	to endure; to bear	5
rēng	扔	ㄖㄥ	to throw; to hurt	13
rúhuáng jrshé	如簧之舌	ㄖㄨˊㄏㄨㄤˊ ㄓㄕㄜˊ	eloquent; a glib tongue	3
rúchí	如期	ㄖㄨˊㄑㄧˊ	punctually, at the appointed time	5
rùmí	入迷	ㄖㄨˋㄇㄧˊ	to be captivated by or be bewitched; be facinated; be engrossed in be enhanced	5

S

sǎ	撒	ㄙㄚˇ	to scatter; to sprinkle; to disperse	2
sǎnwén	散文	ㄙㄢˇㄨㄣˊ	prose; essays	14
sànbù	散步	ㄙㄢˋㄅㄨˋ	a stroll; to take a walk	15
shājī chiǔluǎn	殺雞取卵	ㄕㄚㄐㄧ ㄑㄩˇ ㄉㄨㄢˇ	killing the hen that lays the golden eggs	1
shālì	砂粒	ㄕㄚㄌㄧˋ	sand; grit	4
shā	砂	ㄕㄚ	sand; gravel	4
shāngē	山歌	ㄕㄢㄍㄜ	the folk songs of farmers, shepherds, woodcutters, etc	19

shǎndiàn dǎléi	閃電打雷	ㄕㄢˇ ㄉㄧㄢˋ ㄉㄚˇ ㄌㄟˊ	lightning and thunder	16
shāngliáng	商量	ㄕㄤ ㄌㄧㄤˊ	to exchange opinions or views; to confer; to discuss	1
shāngshāng	湯湯	ㄕㄤ ㄕㄤ	(water) flowing turbulently; (of current) rushing	16
shǎngguāng	賞光	ㄕㄤˇ ㄍㄨㄤ	to honour me (someone or some place) with your presence (formal) or company	5
shàngkě	尚可	ㄕㄤˋ ㄎㄜˇ	passable; acceptable	3
shāu	燒	ㄕㄠ	to burn	9
shèdì	舍弟	ㄕㄜˋ ㄉㄧˋ	my younger brother	5
shèjì	設計	ㄕㄜˋ ㄐㄧˋ	to plan; to design; a design	9
shèbèi	設備	ㄕㄜˋ ㄅㄟˋ	facilities; equipment	11
shéishr shéifēi	誰是誰非	ㄕㄟˊ ㄕˋ ㄕㄟˊ ㄈㄟ	who is right and who is wrong	13
shēnchū	伸出	ㄕㄣ ㄔㄨ	to extend; to stretch out	4
shénshiān	神仙	ㄕㄣˊ ㄒㄧㄢ	celestial being; a supernatural being; an immortal; a fairy	4
shénchí	神奇	ㄕㄣˊ ㄑㄧˊ	mysterious; wondrous; marvelous	17
shén-núng	神農	ㄕㄣˊ ㄋㄨㄥˊ	the legendary ruler who introduced agriculture and herbal medicine	18
shēng	生	ㄕㄥ	raw; uncooked	5
shēngchián	生前	ㄕㄥ ㄑㄧㄢˊ	during one's lifetime	10
shēngdiàu	聲調	ㄕㄥ ㄉㄧㄠˋ	the tone of a voice	14
shēngkǒu	牲口	ㄕㄥ ㄎㄡˇ	livestock	7

附錄四 297

shīyǐn	吸引	ㄒㄧ ㄧㄣˇ	to attract; to entice	2
shīlàn	稀爛	ㄒㄧ ㄌㄢˋ	pulpified; like paste; crumbled	11
shīchí	稀奇	ㄒㄧ ㄑㄧˊ	rare; unusual	13
shīhú	西湖	ㄒㄧ ㄏㄨˊ	the West Lake, a well-known scenic and historical area in Háng-jōu	14
Shī Tzˇ	西子	ㄒㄧ ㄗˇ	a famous beauty of the Spring and Autumn Period; sometimes called 西施 (ㄒㄧ ㄕ; Shī Shr)	14
shìnùng	戲弄	ㄒㄧˋ ㄋㄨㄥˋ	to play a practical joke on; to make fun of	5
shìjiā pínjiuě	細加品嚐	ㄒㄧˋ ㄐㄧㄚ ㄆㄧㄣˇ ㄐㄩㄝˊ	careful and meticulous appraisal and tasting	7
shiā	蝦	ㄒㄧㄚ	a shrimp	12
shiàtiěˇ tz	下帖子	ㄒㄧㄚˋ ㄊㄧㄝˇ·ㄗ	to give an invitation	5
shiānwáng	先王	ㄒㄧㄢ ㄨㄤˊ	the late king	9
shiānchí	掀起	ㄒㄧㄢ ㄑㄧˊ	to lift up; to stir; to cause; to rise	9
shiánjìng	嫻靜	ㄒㄧㄢˊ ㄐㄧㄥˋ	refined and serene; quiet and refined (woman)	2
shián	嫌	ㄒㄧㄢˊ	to be unsatisfied with (something)	4
shián	絃	ㄒㄧㄢˊ	a cord; the string of a musical instrument	16
shiánhuà	閒話	ㄒㄧㄢˊ ㄏㄨㄚˋ	idle talk	5

shiánjiū	閒居	ㄒㄧㄢˊㄐㄩ	to lead an idle, leisurely and relaxed life	19
shiǎndé	顯得	ㄒㄧㄢˇㄉㄜˊ	to look; to appear	3
shiànjr̀	限制	ㄒㄧㄢˋㄓˋ	to restrict; to set; to limit to; restrictions; control	1
shiànmù	羨慕	ㄒㄧㄢˋㄇㄨˋ	to envy; to admire	8
shiāngdàu	香稻	ㄒㄧㄤㄉㄠˋ	rice (poetical)	3
shiāngbǐ	相比	ㄒㄧㄤㄅㄧˇ	to compare with each other; to make a comparison	8
shiāngdāng	相當	ㄒㄧㄤㄉㄤ	very; quite; considerable	11
shiāngyí	相宜	ㄒㄧㄤㄧˊ	suitable; fitting	14
shiāngpèi	相配	ㄒㄧㄤㄆㄟˋ	to match each other	20
shiāngtúng	相同	ㄒㄧㄤㄊㄨㄥˊ	same; similar	5
shiǎngtūngle	想通了	ㄒㄧㄤˇㄊㄨㄥ·ㄌㄜ	to have found the answer to a problem; to have figured it out	6
shiǎngliàng	響亮	ㄒㄧㄤˇㄌㄧㄤˋ	loud and clear	10
shiāuyáutzừtzài	逍遥自在	ㄒㄧㄠㄧㄠˊㄗˋㄗㄞˋ	to wander about freely and happily; to enjoy an unrestrained, happy and leisurely life carefree	6
shiǎudùng	小洞	ㄒㄧㄠˇㄉㄨㄥˋ	a small hole or cave	6
shiǎumài	小麥	ㄒㄧㄠˇㄇㄞˋ	wheat	8
shiǎumàilì	小麥粒	ㄒㄧㄠˇㄇㄞˋㄌㄧˋ	a grain of wheat	8

shiǎujèn	小鎮	ㄒㄧㄠˇ ㄓㄣˋ	a town (bigger than a village, smaller than city)	10
shiǎutōu	小偷	ㄒㄧㄠˇ ㄊㄡ	a thief	12
shiǎuhuǒ tz	小伙子	ㄒㄧㄠˇ ㄏㄨㄛˇ·ㄗ	young guy	20
shīnkuǎn shr̀	新款式	ㄒㄧㄣ ㄎㄨㄢˇ ㄕˋ	the latest ; the newest style	1
shīnshǎng	欣賞	ㄒㄧㄣ ㄕㄤˇ	to appreciate ; to admire ; to enjoy	2
shīnlíng	心靈	ㄒㄧㄣ ㄌㄧㄥˊ	mind ; spirit ; spiritual ; mental	16
shīn shīn kǔkǔde	辛辛苦苦地	ㄒㄧㄣ ㄒㄧㄣ ㄎㄨˇ ㄎㄨˇ·ㄉㄜ	laboriously ; with great efforts	7
shīngchióu	星球	ㄒㄧㄥ ㄑㄧㄡˊ	planets ; stars	8
shíngrén	行人	ㄒㄧㄥˊ ㄖㄣˊ	a pedestrian ; a person proceeding on foot	7
shìngshù	杏樹	ㄒㄧㄥˋ ㄕㄨˋ	an apricot tree	13
shioùhuā jēn	繡花針	ㄒㄧㄡˋ ㄏㄨㄚ ㄓㄣ	needle used to embroider	2
shioùtsái	秀才	ㄒㄧㄡˋ ㄘㄞˊ	a scholar ; the lowest degree conferred upon successful candidates under the civil service examination system of the Míng and Chīng Dynasties	19
shiùmù cháng	畜牧場	ㄒㄩˋ ㄇㄨˋ ㄔㄤˊ	a livestock farm	11
shiuěhuā	雪花	ㄒㄩㄝˇ	snowflakes	20

附　錄　四　299

		ㄏㄨㄚ		
shiuebai	雪白	ㄒㄩㄝˋㄅㄞˊ	snow-white; snowy	5
shiun chiou	尋求	ㄒㄩㄣˊ ㄑㄧㄡˊ	to seek; to try; to get	10
shiunshr̀	巡視	ㄒㄩㄣˊㄕˋ	to inspect (usually said of ranking officials)	17
shiūng meng	兇猛	ㄒㄩㄥ ㄇㄥˇ	fierce; violent	18
shiúng juàng	雄壯	ㄒㄩㄥˊ ㄓㄨㄤˋ	powerful; strong; virile; martial	16
shouru	收入	ㄕㄡ ㄖㄨˋ	income; earnings	1
shoutzú wútsuò	手足無措	ㄕㄡˇㄗㄨˊ ㄨˊㄘㄨㄛˋ	be at a loss what to do; all in a fluster	7
shǒubèi	手臂	ㄕㄡˇㄅㄟˋ	the arm from the wrist up	20
shǒu	首	ㄕㄡˇ	measure word for poems, songs, etc	14
shoushāng	受傷	ㄕㄡˋㄕㄤ	to be wounded; to be injured	13
shr̄dàng	失當	ㄕ ㄉㄤˋ	improper; improperly	7
shr̄diàu	失掉	ㄕ ㄉㄧㄠˋ	to lose (a chance, faith, confidence, courage,etc)	17
shr̄	濕	ㄕ	wet; damp; moist; to get wet	9
shr̄	詩	ㄕ	poem; poetry	14
shr̄pian	詩篇	ㄕ ㄆㄧㄢ	poem	14
shr̄tz	獅子	ㄕ·ㄗ	lion(s)	18
shŕmáu	時髦	ㄕˊ ㄇㄠˊ	fashionable; stylish; vogue	1
shŕjř	食指	ㄕˊ ㄓˇ	index finger	4
shŕbǎn	石板	ㄕˊ ㄅㄢˇ	a stone slab; a slate	9
shŕféng	石縫	ㄕˊ ㄈㄥˊ	a crevice between rocks or in	15

附　錄　四　301

			a rock	
shŕlicháng ting	十里長亭	ㄕˊ ㄌㄧˇ ㄔㄤˊ ㄊㄧㄥˊ	small pavilions every 10 lǐ for travelers to rest	20
shr̀fēi	是非	ㄕˋ ㄈㄟ	right and wrong	13
shr̀shiān	事先	ㄕˋ ㄒㄧㄢ	prior to the event; at the outset	2
shr̀tàn	試探	ㄕˋ ㄊㄢˋ	to test; to fathom; to sound out	4
shr̀fàng	釋放	ㄕˋ ㄈㄤˋ	to set free; to release	11
shūshūfúfú	舒舒服服	ㄕㄨ ㄕㄨ ㄈㄨˊ ㄈㄨˊ	very comfortable	7
shū	輸	ㄕㄨ	to lose	19
shūfā	抒發	ㄕㄨ ㄈㄚ	to express; to give expression to	19
shǔyú	屬於	ㄕㄨˇ ㄩˊ	to belong to	15
shùtsúng	樹叢	ㄕㄨˋ ㄘㄨㄥˊ	a grove of trees	6
sōu	搜	ㄙㄡ	to search	3
sōugòu	搜購	ㄙㄡ ㄍㄡˋ	to collect; select for purchase (a large amount of goods from many different sources, a rare item difficult to find, etc)	3
sūdūngpō	蘇東坡	ㄙㄨ ㄉㄨㄥ ㄆㄛ	(1036–1101 A.D.) Statesman (rising to the position of minister of rites and education) Scholar and artist. His poems, essays, lyrics, Calligraphy and silk paintings	5

			were all very famous	
sūgūngtí	蘇公堤	ㄙㄨ ㄍㄨㄥ ㄊㄧˊ	the name of the dike built on The West Lake (西湖) by Sū Dūng-pō (蘇東坡), when he was magistrate for Háng-jōu (杭州)	14
suéiyì	隨意	ㄙㄨㄟˊ ㄧˋ	according to your wish; as you like it; to act as one pleases	4
suèi	碎	ㄙㄨㄟˋ	broken; smashed	11
suénshr̄	損失	ㄙㄨㄣˇ ㄕ	losses; casualty	18
sūngbǎi	松柏	ㄙㄨㄥ ㄅㄞˇ	pine; fir; conifers.	10
sùngcháu	宋朝	ㄙㄨㄥˋ ㄔㄠˊ	The Sùng Dynasty (960–1279 A.D.)	14
suǒ	所	ㄙㄨㄛˇ	measure word for schools, charity institutes, etc	11
suǒyǒu	所有	ㄙㄨㄛˇ ㄧㄡˇ	possessions; belongings; own; all; to own; to possess	12
sz̄shiǎng	思想	ㄙ ㄒㄧㄤˇ	thoughts; ideas; thinking	15
szyǎng	飼養	ㄙˋ ㄧㄤˇ	to raise; to breed	3
szhū	似乎	ㄙˋ ㄏㄨ	it seems or appears that	7
szjōu	四周	ㄙˋ ㄓㄡ	on all sides; all around; surroundings	9
szjì	四季	ㄙˋ ㄐㄧˋ	the four seasons	15

T

tái	擡	ㄊㄞˊ	to lift; to raise	7
táishān	台山	ㄊㄞˊ ㄕㄢ	an area in Guǎng-dūng (廣東省)	19

tàikūng	太空	ㄊㄞˋㄎㄨㄥ	space	8
tàishǒu	太守	ㄊㄞˋㄕㄡˇ	warden; magistrate (goverrner) of a perfecture	14
Tài Shān	泰山	ㄊㄞˋㄕㄢ	located in Shān Dūng (山東), one of the Five Sacred Mountains	16
tānshīn	貪心	ㄊㄢㄒㄧㄣ	greedy	4
tānlán	貪婪	ㄊㄢㄌㄢˊ	greed; covetousness	6
tán	彈	ㄊㄢˊ	to play (a piano or a stringed instrument)	16
táuhuā	桃花	ㄊㄠˊㄏㄨㄚ	the peach blossom (often used to symbolize Spring)	14
táutsuàn wútzūng	逃竄無蹤	ㄊㄠˊㄘㄨㄢˋㄨˊㄗㄨㄥ	to disperse and flee, leaving no trace	17
tǎu	討	ㄊㄠˇ	to elicit; to ask for; to get; to incur	2
tǎuyàn	討厭	ㄊㄠˇㄧㄢˋ	to dislike; to feel annoyed; irritated; to be weary of; to hate. 1)disagreeable; disgusting; repugnant. 2)troublesome; hard to handle; nasty	2
tǎuluèn	討論	ㄊㄠˇㄌㄨㄣˋ	to discuss	10
téng	疼	ㄊㄥˊ	to be fond (of a child)	20
téngài	疼愛	ㄊㄥˊㄞˋ	to be fond of (a child)	7
tītián	梯田	ㄊㄧㄊㄧㄢˊ	rice terraces	16
tiāntsái	天才	ㄊㄧㄢㄘㄞˊ	a genius; genius	3
tiānhòu	天候	ㄊㄧㄢㄏㄡˋ	the weather	12
tiānshŕ	天時	ㄊㄧㄢㄕˊ	the climate; the weather;	12

			the time	
tiānshén	天神	ㄊㄧㄢ ㄕㄣˊ	heavenly deities	18
tīngtsúng	聽從	ㄊㄧㄥ ㄘㄨㄥˊ	to obey; to listen to; be obedient to	2
tōu	偷	ㄊㄡ	to steal	12
tōuchiè	偷竊	ㄊㄡ ㄑㄧㄝˋ	to steal; stealing	12
tōutiān jȓfù	偷天致富	ㄊㄡ ㄊㄧㄢ ㄓˋ ㄈㄨˋ	to use natural resources to make a fortune	12
tsāi	猜	ㄘㄞ	to guess	9
tsái	財	ㄘㄞˊ	wealth; riches	11
tsáichǎn	財產	ㄘㄞˊ ㄔㄢˇ	property	11
tsáng	藏	ㄘㄤˊ	to hide; to conceal; to store; to hoard	2
tsū	粗	ㄘㄨ	thick; coarse; rough; crude	7
tsù	簇	ㄘㄨˋ	a cluster	18
tsuéntsài	存在	ㄘㄨㄣˊ ㄗㄞˋ	to exist; existence	1
tsúng shēng	叢生	ㄘㄨㄥˊ ㄕㄥ	lush and dense growth; grow thickly	18
tsuòshȓ	措施	ㄘㄨㄛˋ ㄕ	a measure (political, financial, etc)	7
tsuò	撮	ㄘㄨㄛˋ	a pinch of	18
tsz	詞	ㄘˊ	a form of poetry characterized by lines of irregular length which reached its zenith in the Sùng Dynasty (宋朝)	14
tszbēi	慈悲	ㄘˊ ㄅㄟ	kindness, mercy; clemency	18
tszˇkè	此刻	ㄘˇ ㄎㄜˋ	at this moment	15
tszˋshiòu	刺繡	ㄘˋ ㄒㄧㄡˋ	to embroider; embroidery	19

túshū	圖書	ㄊㄨˊㄕㄨ	maps, charts and books	17
túshā	屠殺	ㄊㄨˊㄕㄚ	to massacre ; a massacre	18
tù	兔	ㄊㄨˋ	a hare ; a rabbit	6
tùngkuài	痛快	ㄊㄨㄥˋㄎㄨㄞˋ	to one's heart's content; happy; satisfied	1
tuō	託	ㄊㄨㄛ	to entrust to	
tuǒdàng	妥當	ㄊㄨㄛˇㄉㄤˋ	appropriate ; secure ; ready	7
tzshēng	滋生	ㄗㄕㄥ	to multiply ; to reproduce in large numbers	1
tztài	姿態	ㄗㄊㄞˋ	poise ; bearing ; carriage ; manner	3
tzyuán	資源	ㄗㄩㄢˊ	resources; natural resources	12
tzsz	自私	ㄗˋㄙ	selfish	12
tzyóu tztzài	自由自在	ㄗˋㄧㄡˊㄗˋㄗㄞˋ	carefree ; comfortable and at ease	15
tzfù	自負	ㄗˋㄈㄨˋ	to have a high opinion of oneself ; conceited	19
tzshuō	字說	ㄗˋㄕㄨㄛ	"Characters Explained", the title of a book explaining characters	14
tzànměi	讚美	ㄗㄢˋㄇㄟˇ	to praise ; to glorify ; to exalt	14
tzàntúng	贊同	ㄗㄢˋㄊㄨㄥˊ	to approve of ; to consent to ; to agree with	14
tzāngwù	贓物	ㄗㄤㄨˋ	stolen goods	12
tzàng	葬	ㄗㄤˋ	to bury	10
tzēng guǎng	增廣	ㄗㄥㄍㄨㄤˇ	to widen (one's knowledge, etc) ; to enlarge; to broaded (extend)	8

tzǔmǔ	祖母	ㄗㄨˇ ㄇㄨˇ	grandmother; father's mother	20
tzuān	鑽	ㄗㄨㄢ	to penetrate ; to dig through ; to pierce	9
tzuàntz	鑽子	ㄗㄨㄢˋ･ㄗ	a drill ; an awl ; etc	9
tzuànjiè	鑽戒	ㄗㄨㄢˋ ㄐㄧㄝˋ	a diamond ring	20
tzuànshŕ	鑽石	ㄗㄨㄢˋ ㄕˊ	diamond(s)	20
tzuèi	罪	ㄗㄨㄟˋ	sin ; crime ; offence ; fault ; evil ; guilt	11
tzūng	蹤	ㄗㄨㄥ	trace ; track.	17
tzuò	座	ㄗㄨㄛˋ	measure word for mountains, bridges, buildings, etc	9
tzuòjiā	作家	ㄗㄨㄛˋ ㄐㄧㄚ	writer	16

W

wányóushì	玩遊戲	ㄨㄢˊ ㄧㄡˊ ㄒㄧˋ	to play games	8
wǎn	碗	ㄨㄢˇ	bowl	5
wǎnjuǎn	婉轉	ㄨㄢˇ ㄓㄨㄢˇ	a sweet voice; very pleasing to the ear	3
wànwù	萬物	ㄨㄢˋ ㄨˋ	all things under the sun ; all of creation	8
wángtž	王子	ㄨㄤˊ ㄗˇ	a prince	9
wángān-shŕ	王安石	ㄨㄤˊ ㄢ ㄕˊ	a statesman and contemporary of Sū Dūng-pō (蘇東坡) who advocated government and law reform	14
wàngēn fùyì	忘恩負義	ㄨㄤˋ ㄣ ㄈㄨˋ ㄧˋ	ungrateful ; ingratitude; devoid of gratitude	13

wēiměng	威猛	ㄨㄟ ㄇㄥˇ	awe-inspiring; imposing; dignified; majestic; fierce voilent	17
wéiyī	唯一	ㄨㄟˊ ㄧ	the only	10
wéifǎ	違法	ㄨㄟˊ ㄈㄚˇ	illegal; unlawful	12
wéifǎn	違反	ㄨㄟˊ ㄈㄢˇ	violat (law; rules.) to contradict	18
wéiwéi	巍巍	ㄨㄟˊ ㄨㄟˊ	lofty; majestic; imposing	16
wéichŕ	維持	ㄨㄟˊ ㄔˊ	to maintain; to sustain; to keep	18
wèitzàu	偽造	ㄨㄟˋ ㄗㄠˋ	to forge; to counterfeit; forged	9
wēnróu de	溫柔的	ㄨㄣ ㄖㄡˊ ·ㄉㄜ	gentle, and soft	2
wénrén	文人	ㄨㄣˊ ㄖㄣˊ	a man of letters	14
wénjāng	文章	ㄨㄣˊ ㄓㄤ	writing; composition	14
wòshŕ	臥室	ㄨㄛˋ ㄕˋ	a bedroom	9
wūguēi	烏龜	ㄨ ㄍㄨㄟ	a turtle	8
wúyōu wúliù	無憂無慮	ㄨˊ ㄧㄡ ㄨˊ ㄌㄩˋ	carefree; without a worry or care in the world	6
wúbǐ	無比	ㄨˊ ㄅㄧˇ	incomparable; without comparison; extremely matchless; tremendous; tremendous determination	8
wúchíng wúyì	無情無義	ㄨˊ ㄑㄧㄥˊ ㄨˊ ㄧˋ	heartless and ruthless	13
Wú	吳	ㄨˊ	a surname	20
wǔtz	舞姿	ㄨˇ ㄗ	a dancer posture and movements	3
wùjiě	誤解	ㄨˋ ㄐㄧㄝˇ	to misunderstand	12

wùchǐng	務請	ㄨˋ ㄑㄧㄥˇ	please be sure to	5

Y

yáchǐ	牙齒	ㄧㄚˊ ㄔˇ	the teeth; a tooth	6
yǎkǒu wúyán	啞口無言	ㄧㄚˇ ㄎㄡˇ ㄨˊ ㄧㄢˊ	to be speechless (unable to reply to a question, having one's argument completely demolished, etc)	15
yàjōu	亞洲	ㄧㄚˋ ㄓㄡ	Asia; the Asian continent	8
yān	煙	ㄧㄢ	smoke	9
yānmò	淹沒	ㄧㄢ ㄇㄛˋ	submerged; inundated	20
yán	鹽	ㄧㄢˊ	salt	5
yánjioù	研究	ㄧㄢˊ ㄐㄧㄡˋ	to make a study of	10
yǎn	演	ㄧㄢˇ	to act; to perform; to expound; to exercise	3
yǎnjì	演技	ㄧㄢˇ ㄐㄧˋ	acting skill	3
yǎntzòu	演奏	ㄧㄢˇ ㄗㄡˋ	(of musicians) to perform	16
yǎnguāng	眼光	ㄧㄢˇ ㄍㄨㄤ	discerning ability; power of judgement; taste; state of attention	8
yǎnguāng rúdòu	眼光如豆	ㄧㄢˇ ㄍㄨㄤ ㄖㄨˊ ㄉㄡˋ	The eyesight is as big as a bean (see no further than one's nose); short sighted; to lack insight or vision	8
yànlì	豔麗	ㄧㄢˋ ㄌㄧˋ	radiantly beautiful repledent and gorgeous	2
yàn	雁	ㄧㄢˋ	wild geese	10
yàngyàng	樣樣	ㄧㄤˋ ㄧㄤˋ	every sort; every variety; everything; each and every	3

yàngyàng dōushíng	樣樣都行	ㄧㄤˋ ㄧㄤˋ ㄉㄡ ㄒㄧㄥˊ	accomplished in everything; master of all trader	19
yāuhe	吆喝	ㄧㄠ·ㄏㄜ	to shout ; to cry ; to hawk	7
yáuyáutóu	搖搖頭	ㄧㄠˊ ㄧㄠˊ ㄊㄡˊ	to shake the head (for a negative reply or out of sympathy)	4
yǎu	咬	ㄧㄠˇ	to bite ; to gnaw	17
yàuyǎn	耀眼	ㄧㄠˋ ㄧㄢˇ	dazzling	4
yělang	野狼	ㄧㄝˇ ㄌㄤˊ	wolf	6
yěshiǔ	也許	ㄧㄝˇ ㄒㄩˇ	maybe ; perhaps	13
yītsuo	一撮	ㄧ ㄘㄨㄛˋ	pinch	5
yīdùtz	一肚子	ㄧ ㄉㄨˋ·ㄗ	a stomachfull; a lot of…; full of…	5
yíleng yíleng	一楞一楞	ㄧˊ ㄌㄥˋ ㄧˊ ㄌㄥˋ	to be taken aback; be dumbfounded	8
yìshīn	一心	ㄧˋ ㄒㄧㄣ	wholeheartedly; having one purpose ; bent on (doing something) ; single minded	9
yíbùfen	一部分	ㄧˊ ㄅㄨˋ ㄈㄣˋ	a part ; a portion	11
yībā jǎng	一巴掌	ㄧ ㄅㄚ ㄓㄤˇ	a palm of the hand	11
yíbiàn	一遍	ㄧˊ ㄅㄧㄢˋ	one time	11
yínù jrshià	一怒之下	ㄧˊ ㄋㄨˋ ㄓ ㄒㄧㄚˋ	in a moment of anger,	11
yìfān	一番	ㄧˋ ㄈㄢ	measure word for taking a look, inspecting, thinking, a trip, etc	17
yìbān	一般	ㄧˋ ㄅㄢ	common ; general	19

yìwǎn	一碗	ㄧˋ ㄨㄢˇ	a bowl of	5
yìduǒ shiānhuā chātzài nióufèn shàng	一朵鮮花插在牛糞上	ㄧˋ ㄉㄨㄛˇ ㄒㄧㄢ ㄏㄨㄚ ㄔㄚ ㄗㄞˋ ㄋㄧㄡˊ ㄈㄣˋ ㄕㄤˋ	a fresh flower is stuck in cow stool (lit.), refers to an unequal marriage where the wife is much younger, better looking, or smarter than the husband	20
yǐwéi	以爲	ㄧˇ ㄨㄟˊ	to regard, to think, to consider, to mistake…for…	4
yǐba	尾巴	ㄧˇ ㄅㄚ	a tail	10
yìshù	藝術	ㄧˋ ㄕㄨˋ	art	9
yìshùjiā	藝術家	ㄧˋ ㄕㄨˋ ㄐㄧㄚ	an artist	9
yì	亦	ㄧˋ	likewise; also; as well	14
yīnchín	殷勤	ㄧㄣ ㄑㄧㄣˊ	courteous (ly)	5
yīntsż	因此	ㄧㄣ ㄘˇ	because of this (=therefore)	1
yīnyún	陰雲	ㄧㄣ ㄩㄣˊ	dark clouds	17
yínchàng	吟唱	ㄧㄣˊ ㄔㄤˋ	to recite and sing	14
yínhé dàushiè	銀河倒瀉	ㄧㄣˊ ㄏㄜˊ ㄉㄠˋ ㄒㄧㄝˋ	a silvery stream cascading downward	16
yíngjiē	迎接	ㄧㄥˊ ㄐㄧㄝ	to welcome; to greet; to receive	2
yínghuǒchúng	螢火蟲	ㄧㄥˊ ㄏㄨㄛˇ ㄔㄨㄥˊ	a firefly	10
yíng	贏	ㄧㄥˊ	to win	19
yōuměi	優美	ㄧㄡ ㄇㄟˇ	graceful and elegant (visual); equisite (auditory)	3
yōuyì	優異	ㄧㄡ ㄧˋ	outstanding; remarkalle	3
yǒuyì	有意	ㄧㄡˇ ㄧˋ	intentionally	15

yúboyá	俞伯牙	ㄩˊ ㄅㄛˊ ㄧㄚˊ	a musician of the Spring and Autumn Period	16
yǔjòu	宇宙	ㄩˇ ㄓㄡˋ	the universe	8
yùhuáng dàdì	玉皇大帝	ㄩˋ ㄏㄨㄤˊ ㄉㄚˋ ㄉㄧˋ	the Jade Emperor; the supreme deity	18
yùjuó	玉鐲	ㄩˋ ㄓㄨㄛˊ	a jade bracelet	1
yù	遇	ㄩˋ	to treat; to meet; to come accross	3
yùdàu	遇到	ㄩˋ ㄉㄠˋ	to meet; to encounter	4
yù	欲	ㄩˋ	to want to; to desire to	14
yuèěr hǎutīng	悅耳好聽	ㄩㄝˋ ㄦˇ ㄏㄠˇ ㄊㄧㄥ	pleasing to the ear; sweet sounding	3
yuánshř shŕdài	原始時代	ㄩㄢˊ ㄕˇ ㄕˊ ㄉㄞˋ	the primeval ages	18
yuǎnjìn jīmíng	遠近知名	ㄩㄢˇ ㄐㄧㄣˋ ㄓ ㄇㄧㄥˊ	be known far and near	19
yùn tsáng	蘊藏	ㄩㄣˋ ㄘㄤˊ	to have deposited; to have in store.	12
yǔngyǒu	擁有	ㄩㄥˇ ㄧㄡˇ	to own	11

附錄四 311

版權所有　　翻印必究

西元一九九八（民87）年四月臺初版

中國語文補充讀物第十冊

中國寓言故事

定價新臺幣　二九〇元

（外埠酌收運費匯費）

主編者	國　立　編　譯　館
編著者	方　祖　燊　　黃　迺　毓
繪圖者	王　　克　　武
著作財產權人	國　立　編　譯　館
發行人	武　　　　奎　　　　煜
發行印刷	正　中　書　局

新聞局出版事業登記證 局版臺業字第〇一九九號（9559）
分類號碼：856.00.009（版）新（2,000）(5.20)
ISBN 957-09-1151-4

正中書局
CHENG CHUNG BOOK CO.,LTD
地址：中華民國臺灣省臺北市衡陽路二十號
Address：20,Heng Yang Road,Taipei,Taiwan, Republic of China
業務部電話：23821153.23822815. 門市部電話：23821496
郵政劃撥：0009914-5 · FAX NO：2389-3571

海外分局
OVERSEAS AGENCIES

香港分局：集成圖書有限公司
地　　址：香港九龍油麻地北海街七號地下
電　　話：3886172-4 · FAX NO：3886174
日本分局：海風書店
地　　址：東京都千代田區神田神保町一丁目五六番地
電　　話：（03）2914344 · FAX NO：（03）2914345
泰國分局：集成圖書公司
地　　址：泰國曼谷耀華力路233號
電　　話：2226573 · FAX NO：2235483
美國分局：華強圖書公司
地　　址：41-35,Kissena Boulevard, Flushing, N.Y.
　　　　　11355 U.S.A.
電　　話：(01)718-7628889 · FAX NO：(01)718-628889
英國分局：英華圖書公司
地　　址：14,Gerrard Street, London,WIV 7LJ
電　　話：(0171) 4398825 · FAX NO：(0171) 4391183

國家圖書館出版品預行編目資料

中國寓言故事 =Chinese fables ／方祖燊‧黃迺毓
編著.-- 臺初版.-- 臺北市 : 正中, 民87
面; 公分.--(中國語文補充讀物;10)
含索引
ISBN 957-09-1151-4(平裝)

856.8　　　　　　　　　　87000877